Y0-AGJ-030

BEING A WOMAN OF GOD

Ginger Gabriel

Publishers Since 1798

THOMAS NELSON PUBLISHERS

Nashville

Copyright © 1993 by Ginger Gabriel

Previously published by Here's Life Publishers, Inc. copyright © 1984.

All rights reserved. Written permission must be secured from the publisher to use or reproduce any part of this book, except for brief quotations in critical reviews or articles.

Published in Nashville, Tennessee, by Thomas Nelson, Inc., Publishers, and distributed in Canada by Word Communications, Ltd., Richmond, British Columbia, and in the United Kingdom by Word (UK), Ltd., Milton Keynes, England.

Unless otherwise noted, Scripture quotations from THE NEW KING JAMES VERSION. Copyright © 1979, 1980, 1982, Thomas Nelson, Inc., Publishers.

Scripture quotations noted NASB are from THE NEW AMERICAN STANDARD BIBLE, Copyright © 1960, 1962, 1963, 1968, 1971, 1972, 1973, 1975, 1977 by The Lockman Foundation and are used by permission.

Scripture quotations noted TLB are from *The Living Bible* (Wheaton, Illinois: Tyndale House Publishers, 1971) and are used by permission.

Scripture quotations noted KJV are from The Holy Bible, KING JAMES VERSION.

Library of Congress Cataloging-in-Publication Data

Gabriel, Ginger.
    Being a woman of God / Ginger Gabriel.
       p. cm.
    Originally published: Here's Life Publishers, 1984.
    Includes bibliographical references.
    ISBN 0-8407-4462-5 (pbk.)
    1. Women—Prayer-books and devotions—English.   I. Title.
BV4527.G33   1993
248.8'43—dc20   93-8060
                                            CIP

Printed in the United States of America
2 3 4 5 6 7 - 99 98 97 96 95 94

Contents

Before You Begin

Being a Woman of God contains the basic information you need to build a strong foundation for your Christian life. Many Christians begin their new lives in Christ with certain assumptions about salvation and sanctification, and then they realize months or years later that the levels of frustration and anger expressed in their daily lives is about the same as that of their non-Christian neighbors. Discouragement and depression often set in. The problem lies with the assumptions, not with Christ.

How many times have you asked, "Why does Mary (or Jane or Susan) seem so stuck in her past? Doesn't she know that 'old things have passed away and all things have become new'? Why can't she just get on with her life?"

Or maybe you are a committed Christian and are just as confused as to what triggers your anger, anxiety, or feelings of low self-esteem. I have spent twenty-eight years on the staff of Campus Crusade for Christ, four years as a teaching director for Community Bible Study International, and thousands of hours counseling individuals. I have come to the conclusion that God intended that the old unresolved hurts and abuses in our lives lead us to new frontiers of spiritual growth. As James said, "Count it all joy when you fall into various trials" (James 1:2).

A godly minister advised me as I began teaching a large weekly Bible study, "Ginger, preach each week as though those pews are filled with hurting women, and you'll be pretty much on target." He was right.

I wept as Jamie told me about the pain and abuse she had suffered in her growing-up years. But the flatness in her voice almost made me believe that her childhood had happened to someone else. It wasn't that she lacked emotion. Emotion came when she told about the anger that had erupted that morning at her daughter. Little Sarah had trouble finding her shoes and didn't want to eat what Jamie had prepared for breakfast. The small problem escalated into a power struggle. Sarah left for school in tears while Jamie stood at the door shaking with rage and guilt.

Jamie told me in anguish, "How can I act like this? I am a Christian. I love the Lord. We all go to church every Sunday. I teach Sunday school. I thought that when I became a Christian Jesus would change me, take away my pain, and make me a new person. I'm not sure how much longer my husband is going to put up with my outbursts. I couldn't go on without him. I can't go on with him either. How did I get like this?"

I began to explain, "Jamie, you were created in God's image with a capacity to know Him in a personal way. You were born with a God-shaped vacuum inside that could only be filled by God, made known through Jesus Christ. When you asked Christ to come into your life, He filled that part of you with Himself, never to leave you.

"God also created within you a people-shaped emptiness. An infant has no sense of self. It takes about a year of nurturing, with thousands of moments of memory traces, before the emotion of trust is formed and a baby has 'bonded' with her mother. It is upon this foundation of trust that all the other people-relationship skills are based.

"Jamie, in your case, you received abuse and neglect. You can't go back and change your early years, but God can create a depth in your relationship to Him that satisfies your deep longings.

"God can heal you. I will be with you as you walk through the process of *awareness, forgiveness,* and *healing.*"

There are thousands of women like Jamie. Like you, they don't have perfect lives, and they sometimes need guidance to find God's will. The women's lives I share in this book are very real. To protect their privacy, I have changed names and locations except where I have been given permission to share specific stories.

Come with me on an adventure toward spiritual and emotional wholeness.

1

Women of Value

He who touches you touches the apple of His eye.
Zechariah 2:8

Have you ever had an old tape in your head, maybe from grammar school days, play back to you, "You're not very good," "You're worthless," or "Nobody likes you"? Maybe it pops up at a job interview or while you are talking to your mother-in-law—an old message of poor self-esteem tries to sabotage you. I thought I was the only one who had that until. . . .

Twenty years ago I began putting together a Bible study for the women students on our campus. As we talked about the needs they had, I was amazed that the most popular and most beautiful girls had problems with self-esteem. They had been convinced from birth that their value came from being pretty or popular. They were also aware that the judges of beauty are fickle. "What happens to my popularity if a prettier girl walks into the room?" asked Sally.

What does it take for a woman to have good self-esteem? Does she have to be a certain height or weight? Does she have to come from an affluent background? Does she have to say the right "spiritual" words at the right time, with just the right intonation? Would you be able to point her out at the mall?

A woman of God has self-esteem. The first ingredient to good self-esteem is knowing "I am valuable." The woman of God knows she is valuable and has worth because Jesus Christ is in her life. She has committed her life to living in His presence.

1. What are some areas in your life that make you believe you are valuable?

2. What are some things you wish would happen in your life to make you more valuable?

3. According to Matthew 10:29–31, what does Jesus say about His love for you?

4. According to Psalm 17:8 and Isaiah 43:1–4, what are some other ways God tells you how much He values you?

The world looks to people, achievements, popularity, and approval for self-esteem. Many people believe that if they work hard enough and can keep enough people happy, worldly esteem will last. As with any other counterfeit, it fades when they quit working at it.

God, on the other hand, *is* value, honor, and truth. God created you in His image to ascribe value to you, His woman.

The voices from the world continually compete with the voice of God for your attention. Too often those voices well up from within saying:

"You could never be a woman of God. Your background is too terrible."

"You do and say so many awful things. You could never be what He wants you to be!"

"You have tried to change and haven't been very successful!"

"There is nothing significant or valuable about your life!"

"Why would God be interested in you?"

Christ Redeemed Women

You have a heritage of women of God who knew Christ personally. Christ was born in first-century Israel among men who thought very little of women. They questioned women's value to society and denied them respect and privileges in politics, marriage, economics, education, and religion.

In contrast, Jesus Christ was more concerned about women's rights and privileges than about His own. Jewish women were never instructed openly—except by Jesus. A Jewish merchant would not count money back into the hand of a woman, lest he touch her and contaminate himself, but Jesus touched women to heal them. On several occasions, Jesus revealed major truths to women first. The Resurrection upon which Christianity is based was revealed first to a woman.

The men who followed Jesus also changed their attitudes toward women. As instructed, after Jesus' resurrection and ascent into heaven, women waited *with the men* for the indwelling of the Holy Spirit. They were equally filled with God's power. Women were prominent and respected in the first-century church.

Women Who Knew Christ

Jesus' estimation of women's value came directly from the heart of God. As you answer the following questions, think about the uniqueness of Jesus' attitude toward women.

Mary of Bethany (Luke 10:38–42)

A key word in the title of this study is *being*. As a child and into a good part of my adulthood, I believed that my value came from what I *did*. I was a human *doing*, not a human *being*. I was like Martha, Mary's sister, in this passage.

5. Mary had the sense of being in the presence of Someone who valued her. Jesus became a priority in her life. How do you think Mary's priorities affected the people around her?

6. Most women put their greatest efforts into the people and projects from whom they receive

their greatest sense of value. According to this story, where do you think Martha found her value?

7. What was Jesus' primary message to Mary and Martha in these verses?

8. According to John 11:5, how did Jesus feel about the family of Mary and Martha?

The Canaanite Woman (Matt. 15:22–28)

9. In what ways can you identify with the Canaanite (non-Jewish) woman's distress?

10. In her distress, she ran to the only one she believed could help her. Jewish men did not speak to Jewish women in public, much less grant requests to Gentile women. She swallowed her pride and went to Jesus. If you can imagine Jesus standing beside you, what would you ask of Him?

11. This woman did not have any of the credentials that you would think someone needs to be "valuable," to be worthy of God's attention. What character trait did Jesus value in this Gentile woman?

The Samaritan Woman (John 4:6–29)

This passage gives you a prime example of Jesus' treatment of women. Men did not esteem women, but Jews particularly despised Samaritan women in the first century.

12. How did Jesus treat the Samaritan woman?

13. How did she react when He took the initiative (v. 9)?

14. By what standard did she now measure her value (v. 25–29, 39)?

15. After each woman's name, write out a summary of her measure of value.

WHAT MADE EACH OF THESE WOMEN VALUABLE?	
NAME	MEASURE OF VALUE
Mary of Bethany	
Canaanite Woman	
Samaritan Woman	
(Your Name)	

Marianna's Story

Marianna was a thirty-four-year-old Christian and the mother of two small children. When she came to me for her first counseling session, I asked her, "What makes you valuable?"

She thought for a moment, then replied, "Well, you know I work at the film studio. This week I worked on three copies of a Christian film and improved the studio's sound system. That was valuable."

I asked, "What happens to your sense of value or significance when you have a rotten week?"

She frowned and murmured, "I have those weeks. I either get depressed or angry at someone else."

I shared with her, "There is only one thing that makes me, Ginger Gabriel, valuable. The same thing that makes me valuable makes *you* valuable. Let's look up Romans 5:8."

16. According to Romans 5:8, what makes you valuable?

"Marianna," I said, "if you lost your job because you messed up, left your husband because of your own willfulness, abused your children, wrecked your car, and burned down your home, God would still love you and count you valuable."

The following week I asked, "What makes you significant?"

She answered, "My two little boys. I love it when they snuggle up to me at night and call me Mommy."

"What about when they throw a tantrum at the grocery store and demand you buy them the Teenage Mutant Ninja Turtles?" I queried.

"I'm so humiliated, especially when I lose it and spank them or, worse yet, raise my voice and people start to stare," she responded honestly.

It took Marianna, a Christian since childhood, six sessions before she finally got over the cultural assumptions about what makes a person valuable. It took her weeks to be able to say, "I have value because Jesus died for me and I am forgiven."

The first step toward self-esteem is acceptance by faith that "I have value because God accepts me."

Marianna learned that her *value* doesn't change from day to day, depending on her moods or the whims of other people. *God's acceptance is not temperamental.*

When the reality of what God said in the Bible hit her, Marianna was thrilled that the God of the universe would love her so much that

- He sent His Son to earth to live within the limitations of a human, while still being God,
- He died on the cross to forgive her sin, and
- He rose from the dead in order to make her righteous.

All of that so:
- He could have a personal relationship with her.

WOW! Christ is the Value-Giver. There is no one like Him.

How to Become a Woman of Value

In her prayer of re-commitment to Christ, Marianna prayed, "Jesus, from this day forward I choose to believe what *You* say is true of me in the Bible, rather than what the world seems to be saying."

If knowing God in this way is the desire of your heart, you can pray the following:

Thank You, Jesus, for caring about me, a woman. Thank You for dying on the cross in order to give me value that will not fade away. I confess to You that I have been trying to live my life in my own strength and from my own limited resources. It is not enough. I am not enough. I need You in my life. I open the door of my life to You and invite You to be my Savior and Lord. I receive Your opinion of me as a woman of worth and value. I will make conscious choices to listen to Your voice and believe Your Word. Thank You for being in my life. Amen.

Christ's love gives you value. The choice is yours alone. He will not force you. If you want all that God has for you, you are in for an exciting adventure! Enjoy being a woman of God!

2

Women Who Belong, Women of Competence

To be disappointed in self is to have believed in self.[1]
W. R. Newell

In the living room of a sorority house at the University of Kansas, Patty had just prayed to receive Christ. "Patty," I said, "Colossians 3:3 says that you are now 'hidden with Christ in God.'"

I took a ring off my finger and placed it in my hand, saying, "Patty, this ring represents you and my hand represents Christ. You have been placed in Christ."

I closed my hand, clutching the ring. I then grasped that hand with the other hand, saying, "This other hand symbolizes God. Patty, you are now in Christ and Christ is in God. There is no way you can ever get out of God's loving hands. He cannot lose you. John 10:27-28 says "My sheep hear My voice, and

I know them. . . . And I give them eternal life . . . neither shall anyone snatch them out of My hand."

Patty just discovered the second ingredient to self-esteem, which is "to belong." Belonging in God's hand is an emotionally healthy state of being.

Blue-eyed, five-year-old Meg, with ponytails in disarray, confided in me when I asked, "Meg, how did Jesus get into your heart?"

She said, "He came in through the hole in my sock."

When I later quizzed her, "Where is Jesus right now?" she replied, "His head is in heaven and His foot is in my heart."

Heaven Is My Home

Some women have two houses. As a woman of God you have two homes. Christ has made a home for you in heaven, while you make a home for Him in your heart here on earth.

Jesus told His followers that He was going to the Father to prepare a place for them in heaven. "There are many homes up there where my Father lives, and I am going to prepare them for your coming" (John 14:2 TLB).

1. Where does Ephesians 1:20 teach that Christ is right now?

2. According to Ephesians 2:4-6, where are you in relationship to Christ?

While your outward person must deal with crying children, downed computers, and cumbersome, ineffective government, your inner person can enjoy unbroken fellowship in Christ, seated at the right hand of the Father (with Christ in God).

3. Does Psalm 91:1-8, 14 indicate that this is a future condition or a present reality?

4. What implications does this have for you today?

Eternal life begins the moment you "confess with your mouth the Lord Jesus and believe in your heart that God has raised Him from the dead" (Rom. 10:9). At that moment you became one with Christ, where He is in the heavenlies. No matter where you are anywhere in the world, you are still in Christ, in God, at His right hand. This is called "positional truth," your position in Christ, in the heavenlies.

The World Is His Workshop

Following little Meg's theology, the Holy Spirit is Jesus' foot in your heart. The disciples had a hard time understanding about the "foot" in their heart, so Jesus told them more about the Holy Spirit that He would send to them just as soon as He went away.

You didn't actually become 180 pounds heavier when Christ came into your life. He came into your heart through the presence of the Holy Spirit. You became "born again," according to Jesus' words in John 3:6–7 (NASB), as the Spirit of God entered your life when you made a decision for Christ.

5. Who is the witness (1 John 5:7)?

6. What confidence do you have because you have invited Christ into your life (1 John 5:10)?

7. How is it possible to *know* that Christ is in your life? Does God care that you *know* that the Holy Spirit dwells in you? Look at 1 John 5:11–13 for God's proclamation on this subject.

8. What happened to you here on earth the moment you asked Christ into your life, according to Ephesians 1:13–14?

9. In what ways might the world become God's workshop in Ephesians 2:10? (NASB)

The Holy Spirit empowers a woman's life with the God-imaging qualities that enable her to do the greater works than Jesus did during His life on earth (John 14:12).

The following verses describe the incredible *competence* of the woman of God, filled with the Holy Spirit.

10. How intelligent is this Spirit, according to 1 Corinthians 2:9–15?

11. According to Galatians 5:22–26, what do you know about the emotional capacity of the Holy Spirit?

12. According to 1 Corinthians 12:8–11 and Romans 12:6–8, 13, what do you believe your gift(s) might be?

(Look in Appendix A for a quiz to help determine your gift(s).)

13. Psalm 149:4 says, "For the LORD takes pleasure in His people." What interests or skills do you

have that the Holy Spirit might take pleasure in helping you develop?

14. What is the role of the Holy Spirit in fulfilling the promise of John 14:12, 26, Acts 1:8?

Conditions for Appropriating the Power of the Holy Spirit

The personality and character of God is holiness. John 16:8 says that one of the jobs of the Holy Spirit is to "convict the world of sin, and of righteousness, and of judgment." King David correctly assessed the problem of sin and separation from God by stating in Proverbs 28:13, "[She] who covers [her] sins will not prosper, / But whoever confesses and forsakes them will have mercy." In Psalm 32, David describes what unconfessed sin does to a human being.

15. From Psalm 32:1-4, describe the psychological and physical effects of sin.

16. David prescribes the cure for this condition in verses 5–11. What part of the cure is the most valuable to you?

17. If sin separates you from experiencing God's fellowship, how can you cleanse yourself from sin? Look at 1 John 1:7, 9 and write down John's answer to that question.

Heaven Is Your Home, the World Is His Workshop

As you sit in Christ in the heavenlies (Eph. 2:6), you can look down from His throne and see through His eyes your earthly reality. As a woman of God you have two homes. Christ makes a home for you in the heavenlies with God, while you make a home for Him in your heart here on earth as you surrender control of your life to the Holy Spirit.

The Holy Spirit's power is available to any woman who chooses to live in a listening-obedient relationship to Christ and His word. What a challenge! What a responsibility!

In a living relationship with the Holy Spirit you will discover incredible power in being a woman of God!

Three Essentials for Healthy Self-Esteem

1. To know I have value—
   because God loves me and sees me as valuable.

2. To know I belong—
   because I sit in the heavenlies with Christ, in God.

3. To know I am competent—
   because the Holy Spirit gifted me with a talent and empowers me to develop it.

3

Needs and Neediness Women Experience

Every woman must live with the woman she makes of herself.

Susan called in on a radio talk show. "My husband packed his bags last night and has left me for another woman. What do I do now?"

The marriage counselor on the radio asked, "These things don't happen overnight. There usually are earlier indications that the marriage is in trouble. When did you start to notice problems?"

Susan thought for a moment, then responded, "A couple of years ago."

The counselor shot back, "How is it that you didn't give us a call then?"

Susan indignantly replied, "I've been busy!"

Our society often dupes us into believing that if we keep busy enough our problems won't catch up with us. In our frenzy to keep up with the Joneses, we don't realize their race to keep up with the Harveys.

Dr. Larry Crabb, a Christian psychologist warns, "An unexamined life is not worth living."[1]

Susan and her husband chose to bury their heads in the dailiness of their lives and let the problems fester. Ignoring a problem hurts less at that moment than asking the hard questions that might produce a painful answer. It takes self-awareness to admit, "I have a need."

Beverly is single. This morning she woke up wishing she were married and had someone to love and protect her. Meanwhile, Alice sometimes wishes she would wake up to find herself single again and not tied down by the constant needs of her husband and children. The desire to be single or married are *felt* needs. The *real* needs for Alice and Beverly (and you and me) are security, peace, and special people with whom they can share their lives.

One day a woman may feel fat and ugly, the next, pretty and alive. Her real need on those "ugly days" is not to be pretty, but to know she is accepted and loved.

The *real* needs in the life of a woman of God are the God-created needs for security, love, peace, companionship, being appreciated, and being needed. A woman of God is aware of both her felt needs and her real needs and does not consider herself "unspiritual" or less important because of that awareness.

A Woman's Real Needs

The Need for Security

There is a security to which you may have become addicted: the weekly paycheck. The paycheck, or lack of it, is a circumstance of life. God's security often involves circumstances. It also involves a strength that comes by faith.

1. Read Matthew 6:31–33. What is Matthew talking about? Are these things important?

2. What might happen to a Christian woman who decides to live as though God's promises are for the present?

3. How would your understanding of the character of God affect what Philippians 4:19 could mean for you?

4. According to 1 Peter 5:6–7, what promise does the woman of God have concerning her external and internal needs for security?

If you trust in God's promises, you release God's power to work in your life.

The Need for Love

I was twenty-three and single as I walked into the lunchroom of a Christian organization. I knew few people and felt as though I didn't belong. I felt lonely and alone. Then God whispered in my ear, "Everyone in here who loves Me has to love you. I have commanded it. If you choose to walk in the power of the Holy Spirit, then you also must love everyone here." That opened my eyes. I went from self-consciousness to confidence.

5. What does God say about His love for you in Isaiah 43:4?

6. What did it cost God to be able to show His love to you according to Romans 5:6–8?

7. 1 Corinthians 13:4–7 is a description of God's love, not yours! Write your name on each blank line.

God's love for me, _____, is patient and kind. God's love for me, _____, is not jealous or boastful.

God's love for me, _____, does not demand its own way.

God's love for me, _____, is not irritable or touchy. God's love for me, _____, does not hold grudges. God's love for me, _____, is loyal to me no matter what the cost.

God's love for me, _____, will always believe the best about me.

God's love for me, _____, will always
expect the best about me.

God's love for me, _____, will go on
forever.

God wants to love people through you. He wants
you to experience His love via other Christians. First
John 4:21 says, "[She] who loves God must love [her
sister] also." God gives Christians no choice but to
love each other.

The Need for Peace

I lose peace quickly when I see the flashing red
light of the California Highway Patrol in my rearview
mirror, when my mom gives me the cold shoulder that
says, "You're in big trouble," or when my child
misbehaves at school and I get "the phone call."
Someone has found out Ginger's not perfect. My
peace is gone.

8. Even though "being perfect" may not be your
   goal in life, how do you feel when people
   find out about a mistake you have made?

9. How will applying 1 John 4:18 guide you back
   into His peace?

10. How will the principles found in Psalm 37:3-9
    help you grow into the adult God intended?

Do you see anything in there that says *you* have to be perfect? What *do* you have to do?

11. How would life be different if you and your friends followed Colossians 3:12–17?

Peace is freedom from anxiety. It is also growth. God intends for His life in you to stretch you into becoming the person He created you to be.

Christian growth is like the growth rings on a tree. Growth is not a uniform thing in a tree or in the Christian. In some months there is much growth. On a tree, rapid growth occurs when woody fiber is actually deposited between the bark and the trunk, and that happens during a relatively short four- to six-week period. These growth spurts create "rings" in the wood that help us tell the tree's age. During the rest of the year, there is solidification, without which the green timber would be useless. Growth and healing are God's responsibility. Your parts are awareness, confession, and forgiveness.

Awareness says, "Search me, oh God, and know my heart. Show me where sin is in my life. Show me where you want me to grow."

Awareness is when the woody fiber begins to form. This is often a painful time.

Confession says, "I agree with you, God, that I have sinned, and I accept your forgiveness for me." Forgiveness says, "You have sinned against me, but I believe that God has forgiven you and I forgive you also."

Confession and forgiveness create the rings. Peace, trust and enjoying the Lord is the solidification.

12. God is never in a hurry in developing your Christian life. He is working for and from eternity. What do you see from the Circle of Growth that will help you be established in Christ and manifest His life in your character, habits, and faithful living?

The Need for Fellowship

Hillary found herself alone and lonely on a Saturday night. Instead of wallowing in self-pity, she decided to have a "date" with the Lord. She asked Him to meet her need for companionship and to speak to her as she read His Word. She opened her Bible, studied Isaiah 43:1-5, Psalm 91, and Isaiah 54:1-5, and spent some time praying for her family and friends. When the "date" was over, she knew that she had responded creatively to a lonely time, and her own relationship with the Lord was strengthened. Take a look at the same verses Hillary read and respond to the following questions (Chapter 4 will take a longer look at how to make friends):

13. How can a God you can't even see communicate His love to you?

14. Psalm 91 almost makes the things you can't see more real than the things you can see. What are your feelings about having an angel guarding you, offering protection?

15. What does Isaiah 54:1–5 say you have? How do you feel about that promise?

Alice's little girl, Lindsey, called out from her bedroom in the middle of the night, "Mommy, I'm afraid! There's monsters in here." Alice responded, "Trust Jesus to take care of you, dear." Lindsey answered, "But, Mommy, I need someone with skin on."

16. We do need companionship with special people in our lives, people "with skin on." What are some suggestions from Hebrews 10:24–25?

The Need to Be Appreciated

17. Can you find an analogy in 2 Corinthians 9:5–11 about giving and receiving appreciation?

18. What does Luke 6:38 reveal as the standard for being appreciated?

The Need to Be Needed

19. What would have happened if Dorcas in Acts 9:36–42 had said, "Oh, I am not important, they don't need me"?

20. What talents, skills, attitudes, and gifts could you share with the body of believers?

As you share with others, you will find your own emotional, intellectual, creative, and spiritual needs beginning to be met.

Your Constant Resource

Susan, Susan's husband, Beverly, and Alice all needed to take time out to examine their own lives. Their felt need for "arms to hold me at this moment," may be the *real* need for God's security, love, fellowship, appreciation, peace, or the need to be needed.

A time out for self-examination includes:

- waiting patiently before the Lord to make sure that you are filled with the Holy Spirit.
- accepting God's verdict that you don't have to be perfect. Accept yourself as God created you.

- knowing that it is in giving that you truly receive.

Examine yourself, and then gaze at Jesus, who is the supplier of both your real and felt needs, is the way of being a woman of God.

4

The Rewards of Close Friendship

"It takes a long time to grow an old friend."
John Leonard[1]

Have you ever thought, *I wish I could tell someone what I really thought. Someone who would just listen and not judge me. Someone who would care.*

Emotional pain probably won't kill you, but bearing it alone might. It is important to your emotional, physical, and spiritual health to find a close friend who stays current with your life.

There were "secret pals" at Mary's church. A table in the fellowship hall was a source of joy as gifts mysteriously appeared each Sunday. "Oh, Nancy, here's one for you!" "Oh, look what I got. I wonder who my secret friend is?" (At the end of the year there was a banquet where secret pals discovered each other.)

Mary, however, complained, "I scanned each beautifully wrapped gift, hoping it would be mine . . . and nothing. Then one week there were five 'gifts' for me. I knew I had seen one of them at a garage sale the weekend before. I took it personally.

"Another disgruntled woman, Joyce, and I decided to be each other's not-so-secret friend and meet for lunch once a month and give each other a gift. This is much more fun. Now we call each other during the week to pray or to share special joys and sorrows. It started out as a selfish kind of thing—I wanted nice gifts. But now I feel a lot of esteem, respect, and affection for Joyce because she accepts me the way I am and shares herself with me."

God Created You for Friendship

1. What does a sorrow or joy shared with a friend do, according to Ruth 1:16–17, 4:14–17?

2. How does the imagery Paul uses in Colossians 2:2 describe friendship?

3. What does a friendship accomplish in building character into your life according to Proverbs 27:5–6, 17, 19?

4. What do you know about human nature that would motivate the author of Hebrews 10:24–25 to write this challenge?

5. First Corinthians 5:11 defines what kind of people you should avoid as friends. Describe them.

My Own Experience with a Friend

I've always been a busy person, and it's sometimes hard for me to take time to do something because *I* need it. But ten years ago I became convinced that the Bible taught that I needed a close friend, so I looked around for several months and found Gina.

Gina and I get together often for breakfast to stay in touch. She became the first person with whom I shared my disappointments and failures in childrearing. I learned that another woman hears you differently than a husband does. Gina listened as I cried. She didn't give me advice; she just understood and empathized with my pain. She cried with me. I cherish having a best friend to share with.

Margie's Experience

I asked Margie, a veteran of twenty-five years on the missionary field, what she would like to see me write in this book. She said, "Tell them how to have a friend. I never learned how to make a friend. I know a lot of people, but no one really knows me. I'm not sure anyone cares."

Jesus was a good example of a friend. What you saw was what you got! He did not wear a spiritual "mask" when He wanted to make a good impression. He didn't try to be someone He wasn't to impress people He didn't like, and then complain that no one knew the *real* Him.

When Gina and I started meeting for breakfast, we laid some ground rules: I got to talk half the time and she got to talk half of the time. In the event of a major emergency or triumph, that person gets to take the whole time. It may sound pretty structured, but it works for us.

6. How does Jesus structure your friendship with Him in John 15:12–15?

7. From John 15:12–15, what do you think Jesus' attitude might be about pretending to be someone you're not, so you can make Christianity look better?

8. I find it difficult to confront a friend if she has hurt me. How did Jesus handle disconcerting information about one of the disciples in Matthew 26:20–21?

9. What does Jesus ask God for in John 17:9–11?

10. Being a disciple wasn't always a full-time job. Some of them had other employment. What priority did Jesus and His disciples have with each other in John 18:2?

Jesus lived out His life in the midst of His friends. Again and again He opened Himself up to them, and when they did not understand Him, He had a natural human reaction. He grieved. But He kept being a friend.

After Pentecost, as His disciples began to walk in the power of the Holy Spirit as He had, they began to love with His kind of love. That supernatural love was a vibrant testimony to the new quality of life Jesus Christ gave those who followed Him.

Paul spoke of the Thessalonian first-century Christians, as they "turned the world upside down" (Acts 17:6), "[Your] love . . . abounds toward each other" (2 Thess. 1:3).

11. Friendship is a skill that can be learned, both by example and by study. Jesus is our example. In the chart below, write down five principles of friendship found in Romans 12:9–21. (There are more than five!) Next to the

principle, write down a way in which you might demonstrate that principle to a friend.

Principles of Friendship

Romans 12:9–21

	Principle	Demonstration
1.		
2.		
3.		
4.		
5.		

God Created You for Communication

Verbal communication is your greatest tool in moving toward another woman in friendship. Without these communication skills it is unlikely that you will ever have a close friend.

There are several levels of closeness as women move toward friendship. The following is a chart that shows the growth in communication in a friendship:

Levels of Closeness				
Distant	Low Level	Moderate	Close	Best Friend
Don't talk. Talk about other people or weather.	Share ideas of others. Talk about information, facts, gossip.	Share your own ideas and opinions.	Share personal information and feelings about yourself.	Share your feelings about each other. You sharpen each other.

12. What level of friendship did Jesus share with Mary in John 11:33–35?

13. How did Jesus demonstrate in Mark 9:32–35 that it was important to talk about the tough issues?

14. What level of closeness did this move the disciples towards?

15. What part of having a best friend seems the most attractive to you?

16. List names of people from your life who fall into each of these categories:
    Distant_____
    Low Level_____
    Moderate_____
    Close_____
    Best Friend_____

Try some of these conversation models on a friend:

"I feel (*name feeling*) when you (*name behavior*)."

"I hear you saying (reflect what you heard your friend say)."

(It is amazing how often we think we understand what a person said, then find out later we were wrong. Clarifying what you think you heard is helpful.)

"Help me to understand more about what you are feeling."

God Created You to Receive the Gifts of Friendship

The Gift of Encouragement

17. How does Philippians 2:3–4 suggest that we women encourage each other?

The word *encourage* is composed of two smaller words: *en* and *courage*. To encourage is "to give courage to." It takes a great deal of courage to live a truly Christian life. I encourage my friend when I pay attention to her life. When I hear her pray about a betrayal, instead of minimizing her pain, I say, "Sue, I admire the way you took that to the Lord. It is an encouragement for me to seek God's will rather than fix a hurt my way."

To encourage a sister is to "catch her being good" and let her know how much her example means to you.

The Gift of Acceptance

18. How does the command of Romans 15:7 apply to friendship?

Some of the most beautiful friendships I have seen have blossomed from a conscious choice to accept each other. Friendships grow from *knowing about* each other to *knowing* each other. The real person emerges slowly, even hesitantly. Trust deepens and vulnerability increases. No matter how you feel God wants you to live your life, someone will criticize your choice. But a friend says, "I accept you and love you as you are."

The Gift of Sharing

19. What did Paul's friends mean to him in Philippians 4:14–19?

Sharing with a friend doubles joy and halves sorrow. You have to be a friend to have a friend.

God Created You for Relationship

You were created in the likeness of God. God dwells in relationship: the Father, the Son, and the Holy Spirit. He created within you a people-shaped emptiness. It is His plan for Christians to have friends.

You may have trouble making friends. But friends are not a luxury; they are a necessity. If this is difficult for you, ask God to heal that part in your life (an old hurt, an old message, an old family motto) that keeps you from connecting with others.

Alan Loy McGinnis wrote in *The Friendship Factor*, "Friendship is the springboard to ... love. People with no friends usually have a diminished capacity for sustaining any kind of love. Those who learn how to love their friends tend to make long and fulfilling marriages, get along well with the people at work and enjoy their children."[2]

Friendship is a word spoken or a deed done at the right time, communicating acceptance, love, affirmation, or appreciation. It is the fruit of time spent with each other. Having another woman love you and accept you soothes the emotional and physical pains in life.

Being in the process of building friendships is being a woman of God.

How to Find a Friend

1. Pray and ask God to teach you how to be a friend and then to bring a suitable friend into your life. This is a process.
2. Make a list of possible friends. Good choices are:
   a. Someone with children the ages of your children.
   b. Someone without children, who would have a flexible time schedule.
   c. Look for a new face in church, someone who may not already have more friends than she can schedule.
3. Scheduling actual time together is difficult:
   a. Decide what works best for you, and try to make that work.
   b. Once a week for breakfast worked for us. I often see women with children meeting for breakfast. I prefer to meet without children, but for ten years it seemed like I always had a child in tow. Do what works!
   c. Stay in touch by telephone.
4. Janelle was new in town. She placed an ad in the local paper advertising a play group. She interviewed prospective friends by phone and then scheduled a meeting. She and that group met weekly as they and their children formed friendships. When Janelle became a Christian, those were the ladies with whom she shared Christ.
5. Look for someone who will listen with empathy and understanding and will not always be giving you advice.
   Unsolicited advice is always heard as criticism.

5

Crisis in Femininity

A woman wrapped up in herself makes a very small package.

Have you ever had an innocent comment from a friend trigger deep insecurity? That happened to me several years ago when I took my first course on Christian counseling. It was taught by a man. He said, "Ginger, I found your discussion today interesting. You think like a man."

To this day I don't know if he was criticizing me for not being more feminine or complimenting me for using my brain. I had no standard by which to evaluate his comment because I wasn't sure what *I* thought about being a woman. I enjoy cooking, sewing, and cleaning—but not all the time. I also enjoy doing in-depth research and writing.

I wondered if I could be competent, Christian, feminine, and still respect myself. That raised the old issue: Did I really like being a woman?

What Does It Mean to Be a Woman?

Alice argued in her human sexuality class at the university, "God made women different from men!" But when asked to explain the differences, Alice got stuck.

Joanne said in one of our sessions, "I'm married and have given birth to three children, but I still don't know what it means to be a woman."

Pam complained, "I feel so incompetent when I try to organize my household. Initiating any change feels overwhelming. Are women supposed to be weak?"

After hearing confidences similar to these all week, I grabbed my German shepherd and headed out for a prayer walk around a nearby lake. With the first deep breath of fresh air, I prayed, "Lord, what does it mean to be a woman?"

Halfway around the lake, my heart heard God speaking: "Look at Me. Look at My Word. I created you in My image. What am I like?" So I looked. Here's what I found.

Gender Identity Has a Foundation in Being Created in God's Image

God is neither male nor female. God is both. Leanne Payne, a widely recognized leader in the ministry of healing prayer, wrote in *Crisis in Masculinity*, "Our Creator, holding all that is true and real within Himself, reflects both the masculine (the initiating, strong traits) and the feminine (the responding, nurturing qualities), and so do we."[1]

God created you to reflect both the initiating and the nurturing in a balance appropriate to your sexual identity as female.

Examples of the Initiating and Nurturing of God

1. In what role does God describe Himself in Hebrews 12:7?

2. What nurturing qualities does God ascribe to Himself in Isaiah 66:13 and Luke 13:34?

Did God Create Eve Different From, Better Than, or the Same As Adam?

People who have a need to control seem to need things to be exactly the same, or if they can't be the same, then one has to be *better than* the other. However, man and woman are simply different. The Bible clearly teaches that God is comfortable with *equality* and with *difference*. In God's eyes, one sex is not better than the other.

3. Look at God speaking to Adam in Genesis 2:18-25. How might God have intended for Adam to realize that woman is different from man?

4. To whom was the command in Genesis 1:27-28 given? What might that signify?

5. How was the judgment Eve received different from Adam's in Genesis 3:16–19? (NASB)

6. How did Eve's judgment (Genesis 3:16) reflect the particular way in which her gender was created to specifically reflect the relational/nurturing aspects of God?

Before the Fall, Eve was busy assisting Adam in the ruling of the earth. After the Fall, Eve relied on Adam to protect her, provide for her and give her a sense of identity. (Her desire was toward Adam.)

7. In what way might the effects of the judgment on women be reflected in Joyce's complaint: "I need a man in my life. I am not complete. I can't live without John [who didn't seem as eager for the relationship]"?

Later Joyce understood that because of Christ's forgiveness on the cross she now lives under a new covenant with God.

8. What secret did Joyce find in Colossians 2:10 that changed the direction she looked to for personal fulfillment and identity?

The judgment from the Fall encouraged woman to search for her identity in relationships: to her spouse, her children, her "role." Leanne Payne writes, "There is a popular teaching that encourages a woman to find her identity in her 'role' as wife and mother, rather than in her status as a person in Christ."[2]

As a woman, you need to base your sense of self on what the Bible says is true of you, not on what other people say you need. Any time you believe that you *need* anyone other than Christ to make you *feel* whole, or complete, that need turns into "neediness." Your neediness sets you up for devastating relationships.

9. According to Colossians 2:13–14, what do you need in order to be a whole person?

Affirmed Nurturing

Gloria commented over lunch, "For a couple of decades I have bought into the 'unisex' concept. Except now I see that it clouded my gender identity and has held me back from accepting my nurturing side. I would like to know that nurturing side of me better, but I'm afraid of feeling unprotected."

"Gloria," I told her, "I have discovered a mentor, a role model of a competent, feminine woman of God. She rose out of the pages of the Old Testament and opened her mouth in wisdom and taught me what true femininity is."

I found that woman in Proverbs 31:10–31. She is an embodiment of all the wisdom in the preceding thirty chapters of Proverbs. Her *value* does not come from rewards or her *performances*. Her sense of *belonging* does not come from the *approval* of her husband or her children. The femininity she expresses in her female body is nurturing, inviting, encouraging, supportive, and affirming. Her life is a visual expression of the nurturing characteristics of God.

10. Who did this woman look to for her identity (v. 30)?

11. What made her feminine?

12. What kind of nurturing was she able to accomplish (vv. 12, 15, 20–22, 26, 28)?

13. How might she have used her nurturing to invite people into relationship (vv. 11–12, 20, 23, 25–28)?

Affirmed Initiating

Her mentor from antiquity knew that not only must her nurturing side be affirmed, but the initiating character traits must be recognized, balanced, and strengthened. The nurturing estranged from the initiating qualities can result in a passive, whining woman.

14. Some find it interesting that a woman from the Bible would have her own money to buy a field. Where might she have gotten this money (vv. 13–14, 19, 24, 27)?

15. Where did she look for the approval and permission to be this kind of woman (vv. 16, 18a, 30)?

(Right now, give yourself a pat on the back if you graciously initiated anything today. This could include deciding to take the kids to the park, assertively tackling a new cleaning project, leading a Bible study, or making a difficult decision. Get into the habit of affirming yourself and others.)

16. How does the Proverbs woman refute that it is feminine to be weak and afraid (vv. 21, 30)?

17. What do you learn from this woman about the essence of strong femininity (vv. 30–31)?

You *do not have* to be like the Proverbs 31 woman. Proverbs 31 gives you the grace, or *permission*, to be whatever God calls you to be.

Is Femininity Feeling? Is Masculinity Thinking?

In some "Christian" literature the "feeling" characteristics are referred to as "feminine" and women are urged to be more emotional. The "thinking" characteristics are considered to be "masculine." Men are told to be more cerebral.

The reality is that these characteristics are spread across the genders. Those whose personality patterns don't fit the female/feeling or the male/thinking models feel uncomfortable in some churches. God created man *and* woman to reflect His own image. God intended both men and women to be both thinking and feeling. A whole person is in touch with both sides.

18. What does Psalm 139:1-6, 13-19, 23-24 say about you?

19. How can Marian, primarily a cerebral woman, accept nurturing as a part of her personality?

20. How can Lois, primarily an emotional woman, accept initiating as a part of her personality?

21. Whose responsibility is it to guide you
     in your balancing of the nurturing/initiating
     in your life, according to Philippians 1:6?

When Femininity Tastes Sour!

Things happen to some little girls on the way to growing up that make them defensive about being female. You may have heard such messages: "You're just like your mother" (disgusted tone of voice). "You're a girl; all you're good for is sex, cleaning house, and serving me." "I'd never have a woman for a friend. They can't think." Women who remain out of touch with their core sexuality will feel resentful even talking about being female and about femininity.

"I bow to no one! I am self-sufficient!" screamed Janie in one of our counseling sessions. This was contrary to the information she had given on the intake form: "My life is a mess. Help me know who I am."

Healing the Female Soul

As a woman you begin the process of healing by:

- seeing with the eyes of your heart, Jesus as Savior and Lord,
- believing that you are complete in Christ (not complete because you have a man), and
- accepting that God created you to be both initiating and nurturing.

As a completed woman you are free to move toward the nurturing self that warmly invites people into relationship with Christ.

Laura told me one day, "My first response to certain events is from the old self, who is still afraid to be fully female. I feel naked and unprotected when I don't cover myself with my tough-lady exterior. But the times I trust God with these issues and allow Him to live His wholeness through me, a strong, safe, warm feeling covers me." Godly initiating and godly nurturing from a female body is being a woman of God.

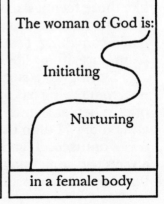

Nurturing is:	Initiating is:	The woman of God is:
Responding	Managing	Initiating
Inviting	Leading	
Encouraging	Competent	
Supporting	Affirming	
Feeling	Strength	Nurturing
Caring	Thinking	
Loving	Loving	in a female body

6

The Forgiven and the Forgiving

Forgiveness is a conscious choice,
not an automatic response.

Have you ever found yourself saying after a difficult or unpleasant situation, "I don't ever want to feel like this again"? I was seven when my dad died after a long illness. I realize now that much of my lostness and feeling unprotected began there. I didn't like those feelings, and I said at a young age, "I don't want to feel like this again." So I numbed myself to feeling anything. I found that I could distance myself from hurts in my life by "numbing out."

Staying on a surface level with people also kept me from having a best friend. I didn't think I needed one. When at sixteen my diary read, "Life is shallow and empty," I didn't know how I got to be that way. I was confused. I gathered girlfriends around me, always had something to do, and did my best to deny that I even had a problem.

1. What would you have said to that sixteen-year-old to help her find a reason to live?

2. What do you think might have helped her become aware of her problem?

Healing began for me when I prayed to receive Christ into my life, shortly after the last entry in my diary. I knew something about Jesus from Sunday school, but I knew little about God's love. I had no idea what it had cost God to send His Son to die on the cross to forgive my sin.

The Jesus Film

Millions of people around the world have seen the *Jesus* film and received Christ as Savior and Lord. Even people whose sensitivity has been jaded with violent R-rated movies still cringe when they see Jesus nailed to the cross.

Most people seem to understand that Jesus is different. There have been millions of meaningless, torturous deaths in our generation. The inhuman acts committed against women, children, and men at this very moment are staggering. Yet, there was something unique about the suffering of Jesus.

3. According to Colossians 1:12–22, what about Christ made His forgiveness unique and effective?

4. What do people need to forgive or be forgiven of?

Jesus Created Forgiveness for You

The thousands of years before Christ, ancient scholars taught morality, justice, prudence, fortitude, and self-restraint as the way to a better life. Buddhism has "The Noble Eightfold Path." The Old Testament taught to sacrifice for sin, but there was no concept of personal forgiveness.

The ancients knew nothing about forgiveness. They could only teach rules and principles to make life more orderly. *Forgiveness is the exclusive prerogative of Christianity. Christ brought it with Him straight from heaven.*

The Debt Against God's Holiness Had to Be Paid

Forgiveness required the life of one who had never sinned to be given for those who had sinned. God is holy, and anyone wanting to come into His presence and experience His love would have to be holy. Christ's dying on the cross paid the penalty for your unholiness.

5. There is a wonderful passage in 2 Corinthians 5:17-21. Read slowly through those five verses. What is the process God follows to make you holy?

6. If you don't think Christianity is making much difference in your life, read 2 Peter 1:4-9 and fill in the blank: If your life lacks the touch of the divine nature (vv. 4-8), it is because you have _____ (v. 9) that you have already been forgiven. What does God want you to spend your time remembering?

7. From 2 Peter 1:5-7, rate yourself on how much you reflect God's image. Rate yourself on a scale of 1 to 5, one being "I never have this," to five: "I always have this."

Reflection of God's Image

a. faith (belief in things not seen)
   1   2   3   4   5

b. virtue (excellence, resolution, Christian energy)
   1   2   3   4   5

c. knowledge
   1   2   3   4   5

d. self-control
   1   2   3   4   5

e. perseverance (the ability to look beyond circumstances and see the resource)
   1   2   3   4   5

f. godliness (look to God as resource for all things)
   1   2   3   4   5

g. brotherly kindness
   1   2   3   4   5

h. love (God's love given through you to others)
   1   2   3   4   5

If your honest score on most of these items is closer to one than five, you should spend more time reminding yourself of God's forgiveness. The more you experience God's forgiveness, the more you reflect His image.

8. Let His acceptance soak deeper into your heart and mind.
   a. What does 1 John 4:16 say that you have to believe?

   b. Think of some creative ways you can integrate Romans 8:1 into your daily life.

   c. Because you have been forgiven, you can write Philippians 4:6–7 on a card, take it everywhere and look at it often.

Jesus Provides Forgiveness for Those Who Have Hurt You

Forgiven love is expensive; it cost Jesus His life. Every sin done *to* you or a loved one, or *by* you, whether you remember it or have forgotten it, has been forgiven because of the Cross.

9. What does 2 Corinthians 5:19–21 imply about your response to the sins others have committed against you?

10. Why would Jesus give the command of Luke 6:28–38? If I won't forgive you, how might that affect my ability to believe that God has forgiven me or my ability to forgive myself?

Marty's Story

Marty asked, "Ginger, when I became a Christian I said a prayer to forgive everyone who ever did me wrong. Isn't that enough? It sounds like you want me to go back and dredge up all that pain again!"

"Marty," I began, "you tell me that you have feelings of rejection, abandonment, resentment, violation, rage, and fear. That tells me that there are events in your life that you haven't really processed yet. Those hurts logged themselves into your memory at the emotional age you were at the time it happened. Then when the fear of rejection triggers the memory, that feeling gets expressed from the immature, emotional age you were when it was first logged. You've heard, 'Oh, quit acting like a baby.' The person would if she could, but the immature fear or anger is an involuntary reaction."

I continued slowly, "Your emotions suggest to me that you still haven't forgiven certain people for things that have happened in your life."

Marty began to cry. "There are things in my life that even the Cross can't cleanse. A little voice inside me keeps saying 'Jesus couldn't forgive that!'"

"Marty," I said, "there is no pit in anyone's life so deep that God's love is not deeper still. You can trust God with your life."

How Can I Know If There Is Anyone That I Need to Forgive?

Step One: Awareness

11. Which deep, hurt feeling of Marty's do you most identify with: rejection, abandonment, resentment, violation, rage, fears?

12. According to Proverbs 20:27, where are you going to find the material to give the Holy Spirit so He can begin to heal you of these emotions?

13. How does Psalm 139:23a teach you to get in touch with your heart, your deepest core feelings?

14. What is the promise in James 1:5?

Even though I was emotionally pretty numb, those feelings came to the surface at the strangest moments. I found that stuffing them back inside without processing them caused a low-grade depression. The definition of that kind of depression is "pressing down your feelings." If pressing emotions down causes that depression, then it is logical that *expressing* them might decrease the amount of depression you are feeling.

The appropriate expression of your hurt emotions will lead you to a greater freedom to accept yourself and others.

Step Two: Forgiveness

15. What does Jesus say in Matthew 6:12, 14–15 to do about people who violate or abuse you?

16. What choice does Jesus give you?

17. What does Paul say about the cross in 1 Corinthians 1:17–18, and Hebrews 12:2?

Many women, after receiving forgiveness for themselves or forgiving the people who hurt them, ask me, "Why didn't I know before that there was so much *power* in the Cross?"

Annie asked, "Why don't more Christians bring their pasts to the Cross? If non-Christians knew that this kind of freedom and release from the old trigger emotions were available, they would all come to the Cross. Why aren't we telling them?"

The Process of Forgiveness

Forgiving another person, or being forgiven, by an *act of the will* (from the head) doesn't usually heal a damaged emotion. You felt the sin against you at the *emotional level* (the heart). Forgiveness needs to reach the emotional level in order for you to be released from the involuntary, reactive emotions that continue to plague you. You were sinned against at a specific point in time. You must remember those specific events and forgive the people involved from the feeling level.

Marsha and I prayed for God to reveal to her a specific event where she had been sinned against. Marsha remembered when she was ten and could almost hear her mother's voice blaming her for the failure of mother's second marriage.

She remembered the rust-colored carpet and the smell of her mother's perfume. I asked her what it felt like to be blamed for something that was not her fault. She remembered feeling shame that she would never be good enough for her mother to say anything nice about her. Her tears told me that she was feeling the sadness and hurt of that event. I asked her to tell her mother out loud what pain she had caused Marsha. (I often ask people to hold up a hand and talk to the hand, letting it represent the person they need to forgive. Forgiveness does not depend on the other person's agreeing with and receiving your confession. It depends upon your willingness to give it.) While still feeling the feeling, Marsha followed my suggestion and said, "Mother, I forgive you for blaming me for your marital problems. Two thousand years ago Jesus put all the abuse, hurt, and wickedness of the entire world, including your cruel words to me, on the cross and paid the penalty for it *all*. He did the hard work of forgiveness on the cross. Because Jesus already forgave you, Mom, I forgive you now." Marsha finally felt the resentment and shame flow out of her.

Step Three: Healing Through the Word of God and Obedience

Healing requires a decision and a prayer:

Lord Jesus, thank You for forgiving the hurts I have caused You and others. Help me learn how to extend that to others so I can know freedom and the fruits of the Spirit. Today, I choose to love and live from a forgiven, vulnerable heart. In Jesus' name I pray, Amen.

Healing for Ginger

Healing came for me when I forgave my father for dying and "abandoning" me. I was healed when I (1) became *aware* that I was still hurt by his death, and (2) finally let myself feel the feelings of betrayal and anger that I had stuffed down inside for so many years. I should have expressed those feelings when I was seven, but I didn't know how.

Many youthful hurts are like that. Old hurts seem silly to you as an adult when you first think of them. "Surely that old slight can't still be bothering me!" But they continue to affect your life, keeping you distant from others.

When you finally feel the emotions of resentment and bitterness and grieve them out, a vacuum is left inside. The empty place provides opportunity for the Holy Spirit to fill you with God's love, joy, peace, patience, kindness, goodness, faithfulness, gentleness, and self-control. By forgiveness you confess your old "stuff" and give God a place to fill with Himself.

Receiving God's forgiveness and love results in salvation. Forgiving yourself and forgiving others and receiving their forgiveness connects you with them and is the joy of being a woman of God.

Barriers to Forgiveness source: the flesh	Blessings of Forgiveness source: the Holy Spirit
1. Need to hide behind a mask 2. Feelings emotionally numb 3. Feeling that no one understands you 4. Events trigger reactions you don't understand 5. Fear of rejection 6. Anger and anxiety 7. Hypersensitivity 8. Need to control 9. Fear of abandonment	1. Love 2. Joy 3. Peace 4. Patience 5. Kindness 6. Goodness 7. Faithfulness 8. Gentleness 9. Self-control

7

Pain and Disappointments

Experience is what you get when you don't get what you want.
Dan Stanford[1]

Have you ever had a sad or hurt feeling surface when you least expected it? That happened to Jane while she sat in a meeting to plan a mother/daughter luncheon. She wasn't paying much attention until she heard Margaret say, "Why don't we turn this into a fashion show and model our old wedding dresses!"

Pow! It came from nowhere, but Jane felt as if someone had punched her in the stomach. Jane clutched her abdomen and leaned over.

Margaret whispered, "Jane, what is the matter?"

Jane cried, "My stomach hurts bad." She left the meeting quickly, totally bewildered.

As Jane reached her car, the confusing tears gushed and an old memory began to surface.

Jane's mother had died the year before she got married. An old friend of her mother's volunteered to completely take care of Jane's wedding reception, pictures and all. Jane protested, but the woman insisted and did it in a much grander style than Jane could have afforded.

After the wedding, the friend suggested that Jane loan her dress to a young girl who was getting married but couldn't afford one. "Sure," Jane responded and left the dress with her. Jane's new husband had to leave for his military assignment and Jane was to follow as soon as she had saved the airfare.

When Jane had her money saved, she stopped by her mother's friend's house to pick up the dress and pictures. She was told that she couldn't have her photographs or dress until she "handed over" the money that the reception had cost the lady. Jane only had her airfare and didn't know how to get hold of any more money right then, so the lady threw out the pictures and got rid of the dress. When Jane cried to her father, he told her, "Forget it! It's only material possessions."

And she did. At least, she thought she did. Jane stuffed the pain deep inside, but she apparently had not forgotten. She had no dress to model or pictures to show her children.

1. If Jane had told you that story, what would you have told her to do with her pain?

2. Has anything like this happened to you? What did you do with the pain?

King David's Pain Offering

What popped into my mind was a story I had just read about the Old Testament's King David.

King David also experienced heartaches. He lost an infant, a son turned against him, a daughter was raped, another son died on the brink of manhood, and David suffered through several disastrous marriages.

But that wasn't all. First Chronicles (11:15–19) relates another incidence of pain in his life.

David's best friend Jonathan had been killed by Philistines. Then the Philistines captured Bethlehem, David's birthplace, running David and his army out into the countryside. David sighed with nostalgia when he thought about "Bethlehem water" and home. David mentioned to his three top commanders, "Oh, that someone would give me water to drink from the well of Bethlehem."

That night David's three most loyal captains risked their lives and broke through enemy barricades to bring Bethlehem water to David. As David looked at the cup of cold water from his hometown well, a lump formed in his throat, and he wept.

That water symbolized all the hurt in David's life, all the pain of those he had expected to stand with and for him but failed. He could not drink. The water came at too great a price. The only appropriate thing he could think to do was to pour out the water as an offering unto the Lord. He poured out all the pain, frustration, and hurt it symbolized to him.

God knows when your offering costs you nothing. He also knows the price you pay when you sacrifice the "joy" of revenge or the "pleasure" of holding a grudge. There is never a time when you are more completely His than when you lay before Him as an offering your anguish and pain.

3. According to Matthew 5:22–24 and Romans 12:1, how are you disobeying God if you hold onto your pain as a form of a grudge, vengeance, vow, or vindictiveness?

4. How do you think the above verses might have helped Jane?

Jane expected her mother's "friend" to act like a mother. David expected people to follow him.

Where Do Your Expectations Come From?

The expectations you place on your adult life and relationships reflect, or try to fill up, the disappointments, deficits, and pain of your childhood. If you didn't get as much praise or nurturing as you felt you needed as a child, your expectations for praise or nurturing today fall on your friends, husband, and children. Your neediness may be greater than they are willing or able to meet.

Stephanie shouted angrily. "They should *know* what I need without my having to ask! I have a right to that!" Expectations!

What to Do with Expectations

5. Some people say that if you love God, only good things will come your way. In what ways is it difficult to reconcile that notion with Jesus' words in John 16:33?

6. What does James 1:2 (NASB) say that caused this outburst from Stephanie: "Get a grip on it, James! Friends? I don't think so!"

The Christian woman who "closes her hand" in anger because of a broken engagement, a baby with a nagging ear infection, a husband losing his job, a death in the family, or finding out that a wedding dress and photographs have been thrown out will find her joy stifled. Bitterness finds opportunity.

Your choice is:

- to do it *God's way* by opening your hands and trusting God, or
- to do it *your way* and close your hands tightly around the little you have so as not to lose it. Either way is a risk.

7. What would you say is *God's* criterion to rate God's faithfulness?

8. Up to this point in your life, how would you rate God's faithfulness (5 being "I trust Him" to

0 being "never there").

5   4   3   2   1   0

9. In which of the gifts listed in Ephesians 1:3, 6-7, 13 have you found God to be faithful in your life?

10. When your personal dreams seem wrecked beyond hope, what is the bottom line from Romans 8:26-28, 38-39?

Choose Forgiveness or Resentment

It doesn't matter whether you call them tribulations, events, troubles, problems, or "opportunities"; pain hurts. The "tribulation" is the activating event. Living on this planet produces tribulation.

11. What does Romans 5:3 say to do with your tribulation?

One practical way to practice perseverance, is to stay current with forgiving others their betrayals, neglect, abuses, and wrongs.

12. What emotional consequences have tribulations brought into your life?

The tribulation itself doesn't cause the emotional consequences. Between tribulation and its emotional consequence comes a choice. You choose to persevere in forgiveness or in resentment.

13. According to Romans 5:3–5, what does choosing the perseverance of forgiveness lead to?

You are only a phone call away from finding out that your world has collapsed. It is at that point you will choose forgiveness or resentment. You can decide *today*, by faith, how you will respond to any *future* tribulation.

14. What is your choice?

Forgiveness Is Risky

15. How might forgiveness release you from resentment?

16. Does an attitude of "pouring out your resentment before the Lord as an offering"

instead of seeking revenge sound like risky business? What if God doesn't heal you?

Proven Character (Romans 5:4)

A person's character—a rotten character, a godly proven character, a passive character, and every other kind—is built up over time. Second Peter 1:5-9 describes God's curriculum at Character University.

17. What is the stated goal of this university and what is the biggest barrier to its fulfillment?

"If I forgive people that quickly, isn't that the same thing as hanging out a sign that says, 'Walk on me?'" Diane questioned. "It seems like every time I start to get closer to God, something awful happens."

"Diane, when you focus on your pain, it seems overwhelming. When you focus on who God is, He overcomes."

Hope (Romans 5:5)

18. How can the command of 1 Thessalonians 5:18, 23-24 bring hope to your heart?

Have you thanked God for your losses, your hurts, your being wronged, your pain? Not thanking

God indicates that either you do not know God well enough or you do not trust Him. You have chosen resentment. Thanking God and forgiving another person does not always make the pain go away, but it releases you from the resentment and anger toward the one who injured you. You can even move toward being a blessing in that person's life.

God wants us to be involved with people, and that involvement will give you plenty of opportunity for hurt feelings. You may even inadvertently hurt others. Those tribulations or hurts can form a wedge between you and other believers, or you can allow those hurts to lead to confession and forgiveness. Releasing yourself and others from expectations and resentments by way of a forgiving heart is being a woman of God.

8

Acceptance of Your True Self

Until you make peace with who you are, you'll never be content with what you have.[1]

J oan was confused when she went to a seminar with her mother called "Achieving Your Full Potential as a Self-Actualized Person." All she had to do was repeat a mantra—"I am a wonderful person"—several times a day, take certain vitamins, jump five minutes a day on a small trampoline, and as a result she was supposed to feel good about herself and begin to earn lots of money.

She asked me, "How does this fit in with being a Christian?"

"Joan," I replied, "if that was all it took to make the old self acceptable, Jesus' death on the cross would not have been necessary.

"Self, having been contaminated by sin, is called the 'old sin nature,' 'the old man or woman,' or 'the old self' in the book of Romans. Living in this old self is to 'live by the flesh.' We are never called to *accept* the old self."

A Daughter of the King

A woman becomes a daughter of the King of kings by way of her new birth. The King immediately gives her access to a true self, and her true self and her old self lock horns in battle. The one who wins will be the one she feeds the most. The only self the woman of God can accept is the true self. This is biblical self-acceptance.

1. Paul describes the demise of the old self in Romans 6:6–8, 13–18. How do these verses help you to know the difference between the old self and the true self?

2. How does Romans 7:15–21 confirm that you cannot accept the old self?

The daughter of the King, who now has two homes—one in heaven and one on earth—also has two ways of looking at her home here on earth. Before she accepted Christ into her life, she had no choice but to dress up the old self to make it look as presentable as possible. But for a Christian to live from this old nature is to practice the presence of the old self.

Secular Self-Acceptance: Practicing the Presence of Self

Many women describe themselves with "if onlys." "If only I were thinner, if only I had a better complexion, if only I could make friends more easily. . . ." They think that if only the right changes would come about, then they could accept themselves.

3. In what ways would your life be better "if only _____ were different"? (For instance, Lucy says her life would be better if her husband looked like Robert Redford and tells Jim that frequently).

Practicing the presence of self is believing that "If I don't take care of me, no one will." It is believing that "It's someone else's fault that my life isn't better."

4. What does 2 Corinthians 10:12 say is the standard that old self used to measure its worth?

Non-biblical self-acceptance is:

1. Self-realization or self-actualization

2. Finding the "inner child." (While "inner child" work is often helpful, the "inner child" is probably not and never will become a Christian.)

3. Self-hatred or self-deprecation
   a. Self-hatred is prideful and very self-focused. If you are busy hating the soul that God loves and Christ died for, you are not listening to God.
   b. If you are self-conscious, rather than God-conscious, you are going to learn how to center yourself on you.

4. Needing other people to tell you who you are or to give you their approval to know you have done well.

The True Self: Practicing the Presence of God

Next to a vital relationship with God, a woman's most basic need is a proper, biblical view of who she is.

5. How does Romans 8:15–16 fulfill a woman's desire to see herself as a daughter of a king?

6. Timothy described God as the "King eternal" (1 Tim. 1:17). How can you relate Psalm 45:13–15 to the life you live?

7. What is the true biblical view of you according to Psalm 139:13–16, Isaiah 43:7?

8. What do the above verses have to say about self-acceptance? Why do I have to accept things about myself that I don't even like, such as my towering height, long nose, stringy hair, or off-key singing voice?

9. How does it become easier to own up to my deficits when I really believe 2 Corinthians 12:9–10?

Biblical self-acceptance is:

1. Focusing your identity needs on Christ.
2. Glancing at yourself and gazing at Christ.
3. Quickly forgiving wrongs done to you.
4. Accepting the things you cannot change.
5. Renouncing any belief about yourself that is not consistent with the gospel.

Failure to Accept the True Self

Until you acknowledge and accept your true self, you will have no choice but to live out of the immature, unregenerate old self. The voices of this world will sound the loudest and you will obey them. Under the power of the old self, you will depend on other people to tell you who you are, to give you acceptance and approval, and to give you a sense of wholeness and identity. You will remain self-conscious.

Strengthening the True Self for Battle

The old self remains alive and well even after you receive Christ. Old patterns die hard. The old self is prominent in habits, tastes, and old messages in your head from childhood about your value, your belonging, and your competence.

Hebrews 12:1a is both an encouragement and an admonition. In the battle to live by the Spirit and to put to death the deeds of the old self, Hebrews says we have a crowd of men and women of faith watching us from the grandstands cheering us on. *You* are limited by time and space here on earth. *The saints* from the Bible who left this earth a long time ago are not so constrained. *From the past they cheer for you today!*

10. What have you discovered about your true self that might prompt this crowd of faithful saints to cheer for you?

11. Look at Hebrews 11:32–40 to see who some of these people are and why they have an interest in your life.

The writer of Hebrews 12:1b recommends that we also lay aside every weight which so easily ensnares us. The extra "weights" hinder you from getting rid of the old self. Those weights are the excess baggage of your past and include:

- not feeling wanted,
- feeling that you don't fit in,
- bitterness and rage,
- a poor self-image that has no sense of value, confidence, or belonging, and
- a perfectionism that resulted from never knowing how high the standard was going to be (if you did well, the expectations were raised).

12. Which of these weights do you identify with?

Three Steps to Renouncing the Old Self

Step One: Awareness

Mary Anne grew up in a rigidly dogmatic family system that felt oppressive to her. Her parents didn't affirm her for fear "It would go to her head, and she would become conceited."

As a result, Mary Anne's self-esteem became as damaged as if she had grown up in any other type of dysfunctional home. When a child's parents are stern, unfeeling, quick to judge, and impossible to please, that child will likely become self-focused and filled with self-doubt.

Other unfortunate things can happen to a child on the way to growing up. A child often takes the death of a parent, divorce, desertion, or the knowledge they were adopted as a personal rejection. Unhealed rejections often surface, sometimes many years later, in bitterness, rage, apathy, fears of rejection, and inferiority.

13. What kinds of feelings raced around inside as you read the above list of weights?

14. In what ways do you see that you have built your sense of identity on the old self?

Ask God to show you where the old messages like these come from: "No one appreciates me," "Why would anyone want to be my friend?", or "Why should I try this, I will only fail." Christ can heal your worst memories. You can begin the process of yielding those thoughts and patterns to Him.

Cynthia confessed to her friend, "I can't believe that I am still chained to these old recorded messages in my head. I know that as long as I believe what they say, I won't be able to accept that I even *have* a true self."

15. What old message runs through your memory most often?

Step Two: Forgiveness

When God shows you where an old message came from (1) allow yourself to feel the pain. Do not jump too fast past this first step. This first step could take months. The more you can come present to the feelings of bitterness, envy, and rejection, the more effective will be the changes forgiveness will bring to your life. (2) Forgiveness is only possible because Christ has already paid the price of the injustice. In obedience and for your own emotional health you must forgive every wrong done against you or against those you love. Memories can be healed from the forgiveness of sin applied to the deepest level of the heart. (Review Chapter 6 for more on forgiveness.) (3) You must forgive yourself for what God and others have already forgiven. Self-hatred is sin.

16. What keeps you from forgiving the person who last hurt you?

Step Three: Renounce the Lies and Confess the Truth

Here's a sample prayer: Father, I confess to You as sin the fact that I have believed these lies and secrets from the Kingdom of Darkness (Satan's realm), rather than the truth from your Kingdom of Light (Christ's realm).

Renounce the old tapes as from the world, the flesh, and the devil. When you become aware of an old, negative, discouraging tape playing in your head, say, "In the name of Jesus, I command that old tape be erased!" Some people wear a rubber band on their wrist when they are especially beseiged by old tapes. As they renounce the old tape, a snap of the rubberband on the wrist reinforces your desire to kill the old tape.

Then take in exchange, the truth of God in the Bible, and build a new tape library for yourself. Listen to God for His healing, positive, true words and patterns to replace the negative ones. Begin believing God's Word now.

- Begin seeing yourself as a woman of God, living from your new center, the true self.
- Begin accepting the things about you that you cannot change. The nose, the height (or lack of it), lack of singing ability.
- Margo remarked, "Others accept my _____ if I accept it. Acceptance of myself makes all the difference. People generally take me at my own evaluation."

17. What is there about yourself that you will accept today?

A Daughter of the King Accepts Her True Self

Accepting the true self is a necessary ingredient to consistently living in Christ. One of the ways to practice the presence of God is to realize His purpose for your life.

18. According to Romans 10:14-15 what was one of God's major reasons for leaving you on earth after you became a Christian?

19. Whose job is it to win the battle of the old self and the true self according to Philippians 1:6?

Come, daughter of the King, into His presence and listen. Fixing your eyes on Him, climb up and out of the old self and into your true self in His presence. This is the true, biblical self-acceptance of being a woman of God.

9

The Man of Your Dreams

As a general rule, a man is about as big as the thing that makes him mad.[1]

If you're having a hard time knowing who "woman" is, think for a minute about how a guy feels about being caught between Rambo and Romeo. Some men feel that women have feminized the concept of love and are tired of talking about how they feel.

Some women demand that men begin to connect with them on a deep emotional level, while others scoff at the "feeling" man and see that kind of sentimentality as a gross weakness. If you as a woman are confused, you can count on the fact that men are just as confused.

Teens, marrieds, widows, career singles, and divorcées say that relationships are important and most want at least one of those relationships to be with a man. Finding the right man seems to be getting harder.

How to Find the Man of Your Dreams

Twenty-seven-year-old single Anna Marie said, "I want a man to have the humor of Billy Crystal, the physique of Arnold Schwarzenegger, and the spirituality of Billy Graham."

Without a pause, she went on to say, "I'm looking for health, wealth, and appearance—and the sooner the better!"

But the man of your dreams is not going to be perfect. No one is. Michelangelo's marble statue of David was perfect. The real David was not. God went out of His way to prepare David to fulfill prophecy, to be the prime factor in the genealogy of Jesus. He told His prophet Samuel to seek out "a son of Jesse" and to anoint him the new king of Israel, even while Saul was still king.

1. How was Samuel going to know God's "dream man" when he saw him?
   (1 Sam. 16:1–7)

2. According to 1 Samuel 30:3–6, what did David do when he was in trouble?

David was a man with great passion. He sinned much, was forgiven much, and David was a man after God's own heart.

What God Looks For in Men

Godly qualities in a man's life are produced by the Holy Spirit and a man's own determination to be who God wants him to be. They are expressed through the unique personality of each man.

Marion told me that she had observed that the men she knew talked a lot about loneliness, and complained that no one seems to listen to them.

Those needs get met in intimate, faithful relationships. Men crave intimacy (as well as fear it). Christianity is about developing intimate relationships.

Personal Intimacy

Don't assume that because a man claims to be a Christian that he knows and operates out of his true self.

3. According to Proverbs 28:25–26, is it possible for a man to know himself without knowing God? What are some signs that a man doesn't know God?

4. The discerning woman needs to understand that the man who hates himself will project that hatred onto those around him. You should not dedicate your life to rescuing such a man. What does Proverbs 19:19 say about rescuing that man?

God gave the gift of wisdom to King Solomon, David's son and the author of Proverbs. Not only was he a student of his father's life (a man after God's own heart), but he was the son of a wrong marriage on David's part. David had Bathsheba's first husband killed because David wanted her for himself. Solomon grew up in a family filled with strife, murder, rape, revenge, and jealousy. The book of Proverbs reveals the pain of Solomon's life mixed with the wisdom of the Holy Spirit.

5. From Solomon's book of Proverbs, fill in the following chart:

	Men to Avoid	Men to Embrace
Proverbs 21:4		
5		
8		
21		
23		
24		
25		
29		
Proverbs 22:8		
9		
11		

From Paul's writings in the New Testament, continue with this chart:

	Men to Avoid	Men to Embrace
Romans 8:5–8		
1 Corinthians 13:11		
1 Thessalonians 4:3, 7		
1 Timothy 5:8		
2 Timothy 3:2–5, 10		

Side-by-Side Intimacy

By nature, most men are more comfortable sharing space than in sharing themselves. Men have relationships with others, but in a different way than women do.

6. According to Romans 13:1–4, what attitude should a man of God express toward his boss? the government? the law? his pastor? the dean of his school?

7. What does Hebrews 12:14–15 say about a man who holds grudges?

Men have a tendency to stay in their heads when evaluating how they are doing in relationships, which results in circular thinking.

If the circle begins with:

A. Poor self-esteem—(lacks sense of value, belonging, and competence) This leads to loneliness . . .

B. Loneliness—(wanting others to *do* more or *be* more than they are willing or able) This leads to discouragement . . .

C. Discouragement—(comes from loneliness when expectations are not met. Results in apathy and depression, and others see it as selfish and disinterested) This leads to lower performance . . .

D. Lower performance—This gets negative reactions from others which leads back to (A) poor self-esteem!

8. Can you think of some examples where you interpreted a man's inwardness as being selfish or distant?

9. How can you help the men you know—father, brother, friend, husband, boss, employee— become more open about sharing who they are and what they want out of life, thereby disrupting their cycle of loneliness?

(For help with verbal skills, pick up a copy of *Lifeskills for Adult Children* by Woititz and Garner, Health Communications, Inc., 1990.)

Paul gave some good advice in Philippians 2:2–4 about being a man of God in good standing with God's people. This is what the circle of self-esteem in men would look like:

A. Biblical self-esteem—sees himself from God's perspective and believes his value, belonging, and competence come from God. This makes him . . .

B. Love others—is able to see others from God's loving eyes and accept people as they are. He then is . . .

C. Seen by others as loving. This leads to feelings of . . .

D. Belonging, value, and competence—he has renounced his feelings of personal shame and believes what God says is true of him. He doesn't have any need to blame others for his deficits. This leads back to (A) biblical self-esteem!

10. What kinds of feelings about himself motivates a man to express love and concern for others?

11. Paul made an impact wherever he went. People came to Christ and many of them became his

steadfast friends. They went out of their way to spend time with him. What would you find attractive about a man who lived Philippians 2:2–4 as a way of life?

12. What might be some difficulties in living with someone like this if *you* were still self-focused and needed to be the center of his life?

Spiritual Intimacy

13. How much of a commitment to the Lord does a man have to make (Rom. 6:13)?

14. Romans 8:4–6 says that a Christian has a basic desire of the heart. What is it?

15. What does Proverbs 28:13 have to say about a man's relationships?

16. According to Proverbs 14:26, what character trait is produced in a godly man? Who benefits and how?

Face-to-Face Intimacy

If you are a Christian, you have acknowledged God as your Father, and He has given you His righteousness. Whether you *feel* righteous or not, this is true of you. If you are in relationship with a man who has not committed his life to Christ, he is still under the bondage of the prince of this world, the devil. The Kingdom of Light cannot mix with the Kingdom of Darkness!

On one level you can have companionship, cooperation, emotional support, and intimacy, but there will be no possibility of knowing Christ in each other's lives.

17. According to 2 Corinthians 6:14–15 and 1 John 1:6–7, what kind of a man is a Christian woman to marry?

18. If you are already married to a non-Christian, what does Psalm 37:3–4 say to do with your life?

The two most important qualities to look for in a man are:

1. A heart for God
2. A teachable spirit

(It is rare for a woman to change a man after she marries him. If you aren't married yet, remember, what you see is what you get.)

His relationship with the Lord will be different from yours. It may be the same in quality, specialness, and depth, but it will be expressed differently.

The Lord promises to give each woman the insight and wisdom necessary to make decisions about the men in her life, "If any of you lacks wisdom, let [her] ask of God, who gives to all liberally" (James 1:5). The following are suggested prayers:

For Singles: God may call you to marriage someday. Meanwhile, ask God to give you joy and contentment in Him.

Dear Lord, if marriage is not in Your plan for me, give me contentment in knowing You and a greater understanding of what it means for You to be my husband. Let me become a woman of wisdom, known for my walk with You. If You have marriage planned for me, cause my man to grow into the kind of man You want him to be. Through his disappointment, teach him endurance and tolerance. Help him become a wise decision-maker and a man of good judgment. Help him grow into the kind of man I can trust as head of the home we will share.

For Marrieds: Some of you feel that you embraced the man you should have avoided and are wondering, "Now what?" God's plan for you is not thwarted. It is still full and good. You might consider praying:

Dear God, I pray for my husband, especially in regard to those areas of his life in which I clearly see You now working. I thank You that You are more concerned than I am with his becoming all that You desire him to be. Please help me to encourage, but not push, and know when to keep quiet. I seek Your grace in our marriage. May we glorify You.

For Widows and Career Singles: Henrietta Mears, a career single, did much to influence people for God. Through her life, her witness, her encouragement, and her discipleship, many others went on to build great things for the kingdom of God. In a prayer like the one that follows, you might pray for similar effectiveness.

A Prayer for All Women

Dear Lord, I thank You that You are the great resource in my life. Help me to be an encouragement to the men You have set in my life. Use me to help them become all You want them to be as I grow in being a woman of God.

10

How God Makes a Marriage

A successful marriage requires falling in love many times, always with the same person.

Mignon McLaughlin[1]

I have just returned from my best friend's oldest son's wedding. Yvette walked down the aisle in a beautiful white dress. Matt sang to her. Candles were lit, vows were exchanged, and prayers were offered. They expect to build a Christ-centered home, filled with the Holy Spirit.

Paul Tournier, in his book *To Understand Each Other*, said, "Most couples enter into conjugal life with a high ideal for marriage. . . . How many of them can say, a dozen years later, that their home has become what they expected of it?"[2]

Conflicts Are Inevitable

"The real enemy of marriage is not conflict, incompatibility, or dissatisfaction, but the unwillingness to acknowledge and solve problems."[3] To some people the only acceptable marriage is a perfect marriage (which doesn't exist). That person looks for oneness in marriage, assuming that it will be his (or her) vision of oneness that is accepted. "Conflicts, incompatibility, and dissatisfaction are inevitable, but rarely terminal to a relationship when faced openly and honestly by partners who want to make their marriage work."[4]

Her Solution Is His Death

John called in to a radio talk show and said, "I have just found out that my wife is praying that I die. She can't stand me anymore but is against divorce, so her solution is for me to die." Many women phoned in anonymously a few minutes later to say that they also pray the same "prayer."

1. What would you say to this man?

2. Read Proverbs 14:1. What are some things a wise woman could do to "build up" her relationships?

Appropriate Commitment Is the First Step

Dr. Ron Hawkins says in his book *Strengthening Marital Intimacy* that the problem in marriage is not commitment. People are very much committed. Each has made a strong commitment to himself/herself.

They enter into marriage with that commitment still intact expecting the other person to help them to fulfill their own selfish desires.[5]

3. What does the Bible teach about commitment in Psalm 37:5?

4. In Matthew 19:16-22, Jesus met a young man who was very much committed to himself. What did Jesus suggest he do to break that strong commitment to self?

5. How might 2 Corinthians 5:14-17 make a difference to the rich young man above and to the radio couple?

God's Solution to a Successful Marriage

Psychologist Murray Bowen points out that when anxiety and emotional tension in a marriage are low and external conditions are calm, the dyad (a system containing two people) is comfortable. The stability of this situation is threatened if one or both get upset or anxious. When the strain reaches a certain intensity, the emotions can overflow to a third person, creating a triad or triangle.[6]

The Christian Marriage Triangle

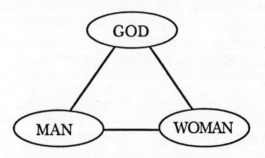

Look at the illustration of an equilateral triangle. The three angles are God, Man, and Woman. All three lines remain equal in length.

6. If the angles Man and God become closer and the angles Woman and God become closer, what might happen to the relationship between Man and Woman?

7. What relationship structure does Solomon recommend in Ecclesiastes 4:9–12? Who are the partners?

God created two sexes. He built into the marriage system a need to turn to a third power (forming a triangle) to stabilize the relationship whenever stress occurs. When God created Adam and Eve, He created them in relationship to Himself, that third party. The triangle that involves God is more stable, more flexible, and has a high tolerance for dealing with stress.

When either the man or the woman turns to anyone else (their child, a lover, their parent, a friend) for that stability, the chance for intimacy and emotional support in their marriage decreases. This may lead the couple to terminate the marriage.

God Builds Himself into Their Commitment to Each Other

The relationship between humans and God faltered when Adam and Eve sinned. In their judgments, God gave them what they wanted. Eve had manipulated a relationship, so from that time on she would look to relationships for her identity, and from relationships would come most of her problems. Adam would look to his work to provide him with an identity, and from his vocation, or lack of it, would come most of his problems. Their sin placed a wedge between them as woman looked to man for identity and man looked away from woman for his identity.

8. If the wedge of sin caused their problem, how can the triangle be a solution for man and woman?

9. The judgment was a prediction of where Adam and Eve's natural inclinations would take them as they looked to people, places, and things for purpose in life. It was not intended as a prescription for a happy life. What does

Colossians 2:10-14 say is God's solution to this dilemma?

10. If your triangle is twisted, what can you do to make it work again?

Marriage Requires Communication

Someone once said that communication is not the problem in a marriage—everyone is talking; no one is listening.

Joanne only agrees that no one listens to her. She said that she was talking.

She complained that Tom had never shared his feelings with her. In a marriage counseling session with them, I was able to get Tom to look at Joanne and say, "I'm nervous about this job. It looks like a new state law might put us out of business. I laid awake last night worrying that I won't be able to take care of you and the kids if that happens."

Joanne began to cry.

Tom turned to me and grumbled, "And that is why I never tell her how I'm feeling. She cries."

I looked at Joanne and said, "Joanne, look at Tom and tell him what you are feeling now."

Through her tears, she managed to say, "That is the first time you have opened your heart to me. Yes, what you shared makes me nervous, but the fact that you did it makes me feel close to you now. I love you."

Communication is the lubrication of marriage. A relationship tends to wear out, burn up, or freeze without the lubrication of adequate communication.[7]

Facing Needs by Communication

Communication About Cooperation

Cooperation with mutual acceptance and respect is needed to solve problems effectively.

11. What do you want out of your marriage? (If you're not sure, begin writing in a journal your hopes, dreams, and wishes until you have a fair idea of what you want and need.)

To solve a problem in cooperation:

- Agree verbally about what the problem is.
- Both partners suggest lots of possible alternatives.
- Find a solution acceptable to both.
- Celebrate a mutual win whenever possible.
- Repeat the process if one person is dissatisfied.

12. According to Matthew 18:19-20, what is a spiritual incentive to work together?

Communication About Compatibility

Compatibility means that you understand, accept, affirm, and appreciate the differences between you and your spouse.

13. How have you been able to support your husband in a cause or activity, even though it's not something you want to participate in?

14. Name an attitude, value, or preference that you and your husband share. Write down an active way to share more in one of these.

15. Building compatibility is a never-ending task. How does Romans 12:10 lend itself to establishing compatibility?

Communication About Emotional Support

Emotional support is important to husbands and wives. Don't try to "fix" your partner or do his emotional work for him, but support him as he processes his own anxiety, fear, excitement, anger, sadness, and pain.

Example: Joanne couldn't stand to see Tom in emotional pain so she felt his pain for him. Because Tom saw her feeling his pain, he quit telling her his problems so she wouldn't cry so much. Joanne finally learned that she didn't have to be nervous, anxious and sleepless for Tom because he had a problem. Now Joanne can say, "Tom, I hear the anxiety in your voice. This must be a difficult time for you. I love you. I know you will work this out." Now Tom feels free to share his heart because he knows Joanne will hear him, but allow him to feel his own pain and deal with it himself.

16. In what ways do you feel your husband's feelings for him, rather than support him, as he works through his own emotions?

17. How does Ephesians 5:33 provide emotional support?

Communication About Intimacy

Intimacy is the kind of sharing and closeness that makes a relationship special. It can be expressed in the form of conversation, sharing of emotions, or sex.

18. What kind of climate could you create in your home so your husband would feel safe in telling you about his deep feelings?

19. How do you think the Proverbs 31 woman won the trust of her husband?

20. How can these ways to communicate answer the loneliness that both women and men experience?

Commitment to Each Other

God has built into every marriage the potential for success. Your part is to make God the central figure in the triangle and to be willing to do some hard work.

21. In Ephesians 5:25–33, Paul paints a word picture of marriage as an illustration of something much bigger. What does marriage illustrate? How?

The commitment in a Christian marriage provides the foundation for a relationship of love. Appropriate communication provides the lubrication for intimacy, cooperation, compatibility, and emotional support.

As both spouses confess Jesus as Savior and Lord, the Holy Spirit can create unity out of separateness and independence. Expecting God to perform miracles on your behalf in your marriage is part of being a woman of God.

11

Submitting to One Another

Your spouse is not the enemy.

Have you ever grumbled, "It would be a lot easier if I just did it myself"?

I have. I have never been a committee person. I find it stressful to work in groups on projects. So it should not have surprised me to find that I would have a difficult time sharing in marriage. And I married someone who likes committees.

We weren't the only ones with that problem. I had just about given up on John and Sandy as candidates for marriage counseling. They had reached the ultimate stalemate. Neither wanted to be the first person to give up any rights or do the loving thing.

Finally I handed each of them a box of tissues and said, "On the count of three, take out one tissue at a time and put it on your partner's lap. One, two, three!" The race was on to see who could get the most tissues on the other's lap.

John was the first to catch on as they alternated pulling tissues: "At this rate we'll both win!"

Bingo! I pulled out my Bible and read Ephesians 5:21: "Honor Christ by submitting to each other" (TLB).

Jesus' Personal Attitude of Submission

As in everything else concerning the Christian life, Jesus is your primary example.

1. What was Jesus' attitude, as seen in Philippians 2:5–11, toward having to live the life of a human being?

2. What words in this passage describe what submission must have felt like to Jesus?

3. What did Jesus gain by an attitude of submission?

4. According to Luke 22:42 and 23:34, 46, what attitude was crucial to Jesus' existence?

5. From what you have seen on TV and in the news about kings, queens, world leaders, and celebrities, "humility" is not something they

do well. Yet Jesus never gave Himself glory. According to John 14:10-11, what things did Jesus talk about?

6. According to John 14:12, 14, how would giving Christians the Holy Spirit enable them to have an attitude of humility and submission?

Example of Jesus' Earthly Parents

Joseph's Attitude of Submission to God

Joseph was handpicked by God to be the earthly father of *God's* only begotten son. That places Joseph high on my list of favorite men.

7. What kind of man does Matthew say Joseph was (1:18-25, 2:13-15)?

Mary's Attitude of Submission to God

For a young girl (or for anyone of any age!), Mary's attitude of submission was remarkable.

8. What impresses you the most from Luke 1:26-38 about Mary's life?

9. How did Mary and Joseph's relationship benefit from their submitting to God?

Shame and Blame Can't Live with Love and Respect

Genesis 3:7–13 is the first example of the first couple dishing out shame and blame. Adam and Eve became aware of their nakedness and felt shame, so Adam told God, "The woman you gave me—she made me do it." This is an example of living from the old sin nature which blames *you* for the shame *I* feel. Shame and blame always go together. If I feel shamed, I blame. If you feel shamed, you blame.

Many a woman has memorized the submission Scriptures, gone to women's study groups on submission, gone forward in church to recommit her life to submitting to the role of wife, only to blow up hours later at an insensitive husband. She simply did not know that, in order to find love and respect, she first had to deal with her own feelings of shame through the process of forgiveness. Christ is the only one powerful enough to heal her feelings of shame.

Guilt says, "I made a mistake," while shame believes, "I *am* a mistake; there is something wrong with me."[1] Guilt can be forgiven, while shame hangs around and blames others for its frustrations.

You cannot respect someone you blame for "the way the kids act." The solution is not to try to show more respect to your husband. *The solution is to experience God's healing for shame.* Shame and blame cannot co-exist in your life with love and respect.

Love and Respect Flow Out of the True Self

By discovering your true self (see Chap. 8), you can forgive yourself and others for the shame they make you feel and the blame they dump on you. You can take responsibility for your own life, rather than blaming others for the loss of who you wish you could have been.

Love and Respect Are the First Ingredients to Mutual Submission

10. What does Ephesians 5:33 command men to do?

11. What does Ephesians 5:33 command women to do?

12. What are your feelings about love and respect?

13. Do you think there is a priority of who should go first in giving?

14. Does your response agree with Philippians 2:1–4?

Healthy Boundaries Are the Second Ingredient to Mutual Submission

By centering your life in your identity in Christ, you will find that you can now say no to unreasonable demands. You can now say yes to God when He asks you to step out in faith.

This is called knowing and respecting your boundaries.

15. According to Matthew 25:1–12, who does God hold responsible for a person's actions?

16. According to Matthew 6:14–15, who does God hold responsible for your forgiving another person?

17. What advice does Proverbs 19:19 offer to the person who often finds herself taking responsibility for others' boundaries?

As an adult you get to choose what kind of Christian you will become. From solid, secure boundaries you will not blame someone else for "ruining your life" or "making you uncomfortable." From secure boundaries you will be able to risk being in an intimate relationship with another person, which is described in the following *poem*.

The Risk of Relationship

Am I willing to risk me, that I might know you?
If I laugh, I risk appearing the fool.
If I weep, I risk appearing sentimental.
If I reach out to you, I risk rejection . . . or involvement.
If I tell you my dreams, I risk their loss.
To hope is to risk despair, to try is to risk failing.
If I risk nothing, I have nothing.
To avoid suffering and sorrow,
I miss out on feeling, loving and living.
By not risking, I live in the prison of my own secrets.
I don't want to die before I've allowed myself to live.
I will only *know* you if I risk!

Anonymous

---

18. What is the level of risk in a relationship of mutual submission?

19. **Benefits of Mutual Submission**

(Fill in the blanks from the Ecclesiastes verses for the first *four* benefits.

a. Mutual submission provides (Ecclesiastes 4:9)

_____

b. Mutual submission provides (Ecclesiastes 4:10)

_____

c. Mutual submission provides (Ecclesiastes 4:11)

_____

d. Mutual submission provides (Ecclesiastes 4:12)

_____

e. Mutual submission provides love and respect.

f. Mutual submission respects each other's boundaries.

Barriers to Mutual Submission

- Shame and blame
- Fear of forgiveness
- Past experiences of helplessness
- Fearing that your transparency would be used against you
- Feelings of helplessness
- Poor personal boundaries
- Poor self-esteem

Breaking the Barriers to Mutual Submission

None of the seven "barriers to submission" need to be permanent. Love and respect are the fuel of mutual submission.

As the result of the fall, many women have a strong need and desire to respond to a man and have him take care of her. Some women expect the man to tell her who she is and give her a sense of wholeness and identity. Only Christ can do this. The belief that men are supposed to do this sets up a woman for "submission abuse" and places an unhealthy burden on the man.

Ephesians 6:12 says, "For we do not wrestle against flesh and blood, but against principalities, against powers, against the rulers of the darkness of this age." Men are not the enemy. Take the hand of your spouse or friend and say out loud, "Your flesh and blood are not my enemy. I choose to love and respect you from the heart of being a woman of God."

12

The Becoming Woman

If you don't know where you're going, how will you know when you get there?

Have you ever complained when you were criticized for doing something the wrong way? You rightly said, "How was I supposed to know that? No one ever taught me!"

Two new parents sat in the living room watching their newborn cry. The young father said, "Margaret, you're supposed to pick up a baby when it cries and hold it close to you."

A surprised look flashed across her face as she said, "I didn't know that."

And how could she know? Her own mother had been cold and distant throughout her entire life. She had no memory of ever being rocked or held in a caring way.

I have heard women brag about their survival skills, not realizing the tremendous deficit they have in life skills. There are many women in your church who don't come from loving Christian backgrounds. Those women grew up in alcoholic homes, substance-abuse homes, homes where there was mental illness, or in rigid, dogmatic homes. They are often referred to as dysfunctional families. Those women survived their childhood because of survival skills. But as adults, those survival skills distance them from loving relationships.

Joyce did not know that there was another way to talk to her children other than "Stupid," "Dummy," and "Why can't you ever remember to wash your hands?" Some of her more sensitive friends criticized her for talking that way, but she didn't know how else to do it. If no one shows her a better way, how can she be expected to know how to do it right?

This was a problem in the first-century church also, so Paul instructed older women to teach the younger women (Titus 2:3–5). Paul left Titus in charge of the young church in Crete to "set [it] in order" (Titus 1:5). It was said of the Cretans that they were "liars, evil beasts, lazy gluttons" (v. 12). Younger people needed to learn honesty, humility, and diligence for the church to survive.

1. What were Paul's requirements in Titus 2:3, 7–8, for an older woman to qualify to teach a younger woman?

2. According to Titus 2:4–5, what did Paul expect the younger women to learn?

3. What do you see as the benefits of this kind of a mentor system?

4. What are some things you would like to learn from a mature Christian woman?

Grandma Was My Mentor

I was lucky to have both of my grandmothers live nearby for my growing-up years. In her later years, my father's mother joked, "If I'd known I was going to live so long, I'd have taken better care of myself."

Her mother had died when she was two, she lost her only son when he was thirty-three, her first husband died twelve years later, and then she outlived her second husband of twenty years. Then, last year, this happened to our family.

I pressed the button on my answering machine as I walked in the door. Stunned, I listened as my cousin Evelyn said, "Ginger, Eva's gone. She died this afternoon. You have to decide about the funeral."

"Grandma's gone!" I wept. My Dad, her only son, had died when I was seven. She was special to me.

The month before, she had stayed with us for a long visit. My husband returned from a missionary trip to Siberia the day before she had to go home. He told us about the thousands of people who had prayed to receive Christ as they watched the *Jesus* film and heard Christian testimonies. When he finished, Grandma Eva grabbed his arm and asked, "Stan, will you preach at my funeral?" He was a little surprised, but of course he said he would.

Less than one month later he kept his promise on the freezing Kansas prairie. Grandma, who had been a spectator to almost all the important events in my life, was gone. Other relatives might have pointed out her imperfections, but Grandma was special. She believed in me. She believed in God. She was a woman of God.

Grandma modeled living through the transitions of life. As women around the world experience the transition of entering the workplace in record numbers, it is comforting to have an "older woman" take you by the hand and tell you, "The future is not such a scary place."

Family disruptions, illness, or a traumatic event may have caused you to miss out on learning some life skills.

In which of the following areas do you need to develop more life skills? In which areas should you ask for help, maybe even look for a Titus 2 mentor?

Self-Esteem

If you are missing a sense of value, belonging, or competence, it will affect your self-esteem.

5. What are some insights you have received in this study about your self-esteem?

To develop self-esteem, you should continue to master skills for work. Find someone to teach you what you would like to know. Look for a group to belong to, where you have a chance of fitting in. Get some art books and practice sketching. Improve your typing. Learn to use a computer. At ninety-three, Grandma was teaching younger women how to do tatting (a knotted lace made from cotton thread).

Also, you ought to continue to master skills for play. Find out what makes you laugh, gives you exercise, and helps you balance your life. Enjoy it!

You can grow at your own pace. You don't have to keep up with the woman next door who seems to have it all together.

Vulnerability With Protection

Vulnerability is your growth toward self-acceptance. You can only do that as you utilize healthy *boundaries for protection* from unsafe people.

6. What have you learned about the need to have boundaries around your vulnerability?

Offer and accept friendship as you are able. Learn how to assess whether someone is "safe" to share with. Risk a little in this area. A muscle does not grow unless it is stretched (this hurts some). Share a few of your "secrets" with a safe friend. Share at your own pace, but share. The greatest pain is not in betrayal of your secret, but in the isolation you experience if you don't risk. Also, honor the uniqueness of others, and support their growth.

Expressing humor requires a willingness to be vulnerable. Resentments and bitterness are often released by a touch of humor.

Interdependence

Interdependence is about admitting to the need to be in relationship with others. The chapter on friendship (4), the one on marriage (10), and the one on submitting to one another (11) talk about interdependence. A mature woman of God is not ashamed to depend on others sometimes or afraid to act independently sometimes.

7. In what way does *interdependent* sound mature? Sound selfish?

   a. Find a mentor for the next phase of your life. (Shouldn't a woman mentor be called a "womentor"?) If your children are preschoolers, begin looking for that woman whose children are a little older and ask her to coach you. In grandma's day, women got together regularly for quilting bees. They discussed marital relations, child discipline problems, remedies for depression, and other ailments. We don't have that today, but need it. Someone who has been there can help guide you in life.

   b. Find someone you can mentor, someone who is coming after you along the pathway of life. You can invest some of the wisdom you've acquired.

8. Who will you ask to be your mentor? What would you like to learn from her? (List several women in case the first is unavailable.)

9. How much time would you be willing or able to give the woman who asks you to be her mentor?

Maturity

I have heard it said that forty is the old age of youth, while fifty is the youth of old age.

10. What does maturity mean to you?

- The mature woman accepts responsibility for her own boundaries. Therefore, she is able to offer and accept friendship.
- The mature woman is strong in her sense of identity; that is, she has spent time in self-awareness. She has honestly faced her needs and taken responsibility for getting them met and has asked for help when needed. Her self-esteem is intact.
- She accepts her life for what it is and what it is not.
- The woman of God is beautiful and loveable at every age. Love matures and expands at every age.

Grandma Eva was a good role model for aging. Being forty lost its sting when my cousin Forrest, also forty, and I lunched with our grandmas (sisters-in-law) when they were in their eighties. They laughed and carried on so, we felt like kids. I don't mind being the

age I am because one who went before showed me
how to do it.

- The mature woman refines the art of *greeting,
  leaving, and grieving*. It is important to grieve
  the loss of people, dreams, possessions, a way
  of life, or a role you particularly enjoyed in life
  when those things no longer can be a part of
  your life. The first stage of healthy grieving is
  to honestly look at what the loss means. It often
  includes a healthy dose of anger after the "I'm
  dealing with it just fine" denial wears thin.
  Healthy grieving takes all the feelings, feels
  them thoroughly, and after a process (don't
  rush yourself) is able to accept the loss.
- The mature woman balances dependence and
  independence with interdependence.

Looking to God for Help

11. This whole study has been about looking to God.
    What have you learned the most about
    looking to God for your identity?

Spiritual and emotional growth deepens integrity
and spirituality. Isaiah 54:2, 5a says,

Enlarge the place of your tent,
And let them stretch out the curtains
   of your dwellings;
Do not spare;
Lengthen your cords,
And strengthen your stakes. . . .
For your Maker is your husband.

Being a woman of God is about being more *with God* than you could ever hope to be without Him.

A Dozen Barriers to Being a Woman of God

1. Holding on to shame and blame
2. Unwillingness to learn, grow, and change
3. Competition with others for emotional needs
4. Imposing your definition of the world on others
5. Passivity, addictions, and codependency
6. Minimizing, discounting and denial
7. Overdependence on others
8. Fear of depending on others
9. Independence to the exclusion of inter-dependence
10. Difficulty making and keeping commitments
11. Fear of growing old, afraid of death
12. Unwillingness to grieve losses and move on with life

---

12. Look at the list of the barriers to becoming a mature woman of God. What barriers do you have the most trouble with?

I had assumed that because I married a Christian and stayed in full-time Christian work, that we would have a "Christ-centered" home. Yet our home life fell far short of what I had dreamed it would be. Between the dream and the reality should have been a "womentor," a Titus 2 woman, a Proverbs 31 woman, or a study like *Being a Woman of God* to guide me.

Several years ago, I stumbled across Edith Schaeffer's *The Tapestry*,[1] and as I read her book I had the sense of Edith mothering me. (Do we ever stop wanting to feel special?) The book is huge because she details so much of her family's life. I felt as though I were living right there with her. Several nights a week after putting the kids to bed, I would build a fire, make a cup of cocoa, and read a portion of *The Tapestry*. That was one way of learning and being mentored.

Give yourself opportunities to be mothered and mentored. It doesn't matter how old you are. *Being a Woman of God* may have answered questions for you. It may have brought up issues in your life that you need to take a closer look at. I love your "becoming woman" and desire that you continue in your quest of being a woman of God.

13

Finding Time to Be a Woman of God

The royal daughter is all glorious within the palace;
Her clothing is woven with gold.
She shall be brought to the King in robes of many colors;
The virgins, her companions who follow her,
shall be brought to You.
With gladness and rejoicing they shall be brought;
They shall enter the King's palace.

Psalm 45:13–15

If you fail to plan, you should plan to fail. Grand events don't just happen. Glorious clothing doesn't appear at the snap of the fingers. Loyal companionship doesn't "just happen." Some women can make it look as though it just happens, but it doesn't.

Time is the great equalizer. Everyone gets twenty-four hours a day. The women who make grand events happen, who maintain order in their wardrobes, and who create harmony in their households all have one thing in common: They organize. They know where they are going, how they are going to get there, and where they've been once it's over.

You need a little knowledge, some training, and a great desire for something more than what you are now experiencing. Whatever your circumstances are right now—single, young married, wife and mother, single parent, middle-aged, or older—this chapter is designed as an introduction to help you step into that kind of life.

For some of you, this chapter will be all you want for now. However, if this sparks an interest, you will love Emilie Barnes's book *Survival for Busy Women*.

Time Out to Dream

The most important place to start planning and organizing is in your heart.

1. Proverbs 29:18 in the King James translation says, "Where there is no vision, the people perish." What does that suggest will happen when a woman or a nation has no plan?

2. What does Psalm 37:3–5 suggest as God's viewpoint on a woman's dream?

3. Being anxious, worrying, and fretting won't get you your dream. In what ways do you think God really expects you to obey Psalm 37:7–9?

The goals and plans for your life have to be carved out of your own dreams. My vision for your life won't keep your motivation up after your body is tired and wants to quit. God instills deep in your heart His purposes for your life. When you have yielded your life to Him, the desires of your heart will match His plan for your life (Psalm 37:4).

4. On this list of dreams and desires, write down what you wish your life looked like in each of these areas right now! (If you are doing a group study, do not spend more than 5 minutes on this in group time. Look at it again later.)

List of Dreams and Desires

a. Romantic Dreams:

_____

b. Intellectual Dreams:

_____

c. Physical Dreams:

_____

d. Spiritual Dreams:

_____

e. Ministry Dreams:

_____

f. Social Dreams:

_____

g. Domestic Dreams:

_____

h. Family Dreams:

_____

i. Recreational Dreams:

_____

j. Financial Dreams:

_____

---

5. Which of these dreams could interface with the spiritual gift(s) that you feel that the Holy Spirit has given you (Chapter 2)?

6. Which of these areas can you imagine that the Holy Spirit would find pleasure in helping you develop?

Margie complained, "But you don't understand. I have no control over my own time. What is the point of dreaming for something more out of my life? I'll never get there."

I responded, "You do have control over what and how much you eat, how much television you watch, how much time you spend looking at magazines and reading books. You have control over what you choose to think about. You can choose the songs you sing to your babies or yourself. You can choose your own self-talk. There are a lot of little spots of time you do have some control over.

"Your problem isn't lack of time. Your problem is that you have never believed God would give you a vision (Proverbs 29:18) for what His purpose for your life is.

"If you don't take aim and try to hit a target, you'll never know how close you might have come to a bull's-eye."

Pray for Wisdom and Courage to Develop a Dream

7. What does James 1:5 promise if you are uncertain as to which direction you should go?

Heavenly Father, right now I ask You to give me wisdom to know if it is all right to have dreams for my own life. Help me sense the wisdom of the Holy Spirit as I initiate some changes in my life. I believe that You desire to do "great and mighty" things in and through me. Give me courage to dream and act.

Weekly Schedule

I have always found it valuable to keep a weekly schedule. While I was in Spain with three preschoolers, I felt the need to work on something just for me. I was involved with the kids and the ministry most days and evenings. I discovered that I could finish up a master's degree in missions by correspondence.

I broke down my time into bite-size pieces and set aside two hours each Tuesday and Thursday night from 8:00 P.M. until 10:00 P.M. I got all the course work done in one year and then spent several months studying for the comprehensive exam. I just barely passed, but I passed!

Begin to fill in the known commitments on your weekly schedule. (Another blank schedule is in Appendix C.) The empty spots on your weekly schedule indicate possible time available to work on long-term goals.

Weekly Schedule for Being a Woman of God

	SUNDAY	MONDAY	TUESDAY	WEDNESDAY	THURSDAY	FRIDAY	SATURDAY
6 a.m.							
7							
8							
9							
10							
11							
12 noon							
1							
2							
3							
4							
5							
6							
7							
8							
9							
10							

Long-Term Goals

A life is never changed by spontaneous gestures. God did not give you His Holy Spirit to wear you out in serving Him. It is exhausting to run around in a circle. Take the time to set a goal, and then steadily move toward that goal.

8. How might Paul have given his approval in 1 Corinthians 9:26–27 to long-term goals?

9. Moses would have understood the overwhelming feeling a modern woman gets from the demands on her time. Moses was overwhelmed. He needed a plan. What did his father-in-law suggest in Exodus 18:12–24?

How to Set Goals

In a couple of years I will be fifty. Because I set some eating and exercise goals ten years ago, I feel better now, have more energy, and have a much better attitude toward life than I did then. Where do you need to be five years from now in order to fulfill a ten-year goal? Where will you need to be in one year? What do you need to do today? Even if you don't hit your bull's-eye, you will be a lot closer to the target than if you had no goals. The goal of this exercise is to examine your life to make your living more intentional.

Several worksheets are included in this book. It will be overwhelming for you to try to organize your entire future in one evening. For right now pick one area you are most concerned with: spiritual, physical, family, financial, career, mental, social, domestic, recreation, ministry, or romantic. (For example, if your biggest problem is with the kids or your husband, start with family. If your household management is a disaster, try domestic.)

Write down the area you will start with. Read through the sample. Fill out the blank form in Appendix C for practice now. (Don't spend more than five minutes filling in the blank form in group.) Photocopy as many of these forms as you need to complete each project.

Long-Term Goals (Sample)

Area: Ministry

Goal: To learn how to share my faith with others.

Activities for Reaching the Goal:

Ten-Year Goal Activities: To train others in sharing their faith by having a lifestyle that reflects the love of Christ.

Five-Year Goal Activities: To teach a small group of women in Sunday School how to share Christ through their lifestyle.

One-Year Goal Activities: To attend a witnessing class at church. To attend a lay witnessing training class.

Weekly Goal Activities: To invite my neighbor over for coffee and begin to meet some non-Christians. Memorize the "Four Spiritual Laws."

Goals are merely directional markers leading you onward. Sometimes I get excited about Plan "A," while God may have Plan "C" in mind for me, but I would never dream of putting "C" on my dream list. It is too incredible.

So He allows me to pursue "A," which gets me to the right location to be willing to consider "B." After a while I realize that "B" is much more suited to my talents. "B" moves me on to a different location where I meet someone from "C" who says, "We have been praying for someone with your flexibility, skills, and heart for God."

I laugh when I realize that not even a hint of "C" was on my original planning chart. Yet I now recognize that "C" was exactly what my deepest heart's desire had been from the start.

God has a plan for you, but if you can't see your way to trust God for "A," you will never get to "C." Goals can always be dropped, amended, even reversed. As a matter of fact, they usually are.

Yearly Goals

Keeping your ten-year goal in front of you, break down your goal into five-year goals and yearly goals. As a mom, your year may often coincide with the school year. In general, yearly goals are often the most manageable slices of time you have. (The older you get, the quicker it seems that the five- and ten-year goals come up for revision.)

Look at the sample and then for practice fill in the worksheet in Appendix C using the same area you picked for long-term goals. As you do your Yearly Planning Worksheets, keep your Weekly Schedule in front of you so as you work your plan you can see if your plan will work. Fill in the time slots with your dream.

Work the Plan

There will be a great social function one day and you will be the guest of honor. People will sing your praise. It will be your funeral. How do you want your epitaph to read? Paul chose for his epitaph "I have fought the good fight, I have finished the race, I have kept the faith" (2 Tim. 4:7). The Proverbs 31 woman didn't have to wait to die in order to hear her epitaph.

Charm is deceitful and beauty is vain,
But a woman who fears the LORD, she shall be praised.
Give her of the fruit of her hands,
And let her own works praise her in the gates.
(Prov. 31:30, 31)

Yearly Planning Worksheet (Sample)

Yearly Goal	Activities	Schedule
Spiritual: to have a vital relationship with God.	Read *My Utmost For His Highest* by Oswald Chambers	30 min. daily 6:30-7:00 a.m.
	Pray daily	10 min. daily
Physical: to have a healthy body	Maintain weight at 140 lbs.	Cook "light" meals
	Exercise regularly	20 minutes daily 6:10- 6:30
Mental: to broaden my intellect by being informed	Read a news periodical	Sunday afternoon
	Read a Christian bestseller	Tues. & Thurs. evenings
Social: to meet people from different backgrounds	Have couples over for dinner	Twice a month on Friday nights

10. What would you like people to say about your life?

Pat yourself, and each other, on the back for persevering to the end of this study. I congratulate you and trust that your life has been enriched. It is your privilege to walk with Jesus as He leads you to carve out, with your own unique life, your version of being a woman of God.

Appendix A

Discover Your Spiritual Gift

This spiritual gift search is a starting place to help you discover the spiritual gift(s) God gave you the moment you became a Christian. This is only intended to point you in the right direction, not to be the last word. The longer you have been a Christian, the more maturity and experience you will bring to each question and the more valid will be the results. This search is limited to Romans 12:6–13. There are other passages of Scripture that deal with other spiritual gifts.

If none of the gifts here seem to apply to you, you will want to continue your search. The question is not, "Do I have a spiritual gift?" The question is, "In which of these ministries has the Lord especially gifted me to strengthen the Body of Christ?"

How to score your search:

The eight gifts from Romans 12:6–13 are listed. Under each gift are three descriptions.
1. Rate each description 3–0, 3 being "I do it all the time," 0 being "not at all."

2. When you have finished, return to the beginning and total the points you have given yourself for each gift.

3. Then rank the gifts to see which ones you scored the highest on.

4. Read the definitions for those gifts and begin asking the Lord to give you wisdom in developing the one that you seem the most attracted to. Begin looking for opportunities to express that gift in service to other Christians in the church and community, or begin to get training in that area.

Spiritual Gift Search

A. Prophecy

	3 MUCH	2 SOME	1 LITTLE	0 NONE
1. I have communicated to others timely and urgent messages I felt came from the Lord.				
2. I have a desire to speak direct messages from God that edify, exhort, or comfort.				

3 MUCH	2 SOME	1 LITTLE	0 NONE

3. I have given messages of warning, judgment, or direction from the Lord.

TOTAL

B. Teaching

1. I feel I can help people to learn biblical truths in detail.

2. I would like to learn more biblical truth to communicate to others.

3. I have trained other Christians to be more obedient disciples of Christ.

TOTAL

C. Exhortation

	3 MUCH	2 SOME	1 LITTLE	0 NONE
1. I have verbally encouraged the struggling, the troubled, or the discouraged.				
2. I have urged others to seek a biblical solution to their suffering.				
3. I feel I could be an instrument for dislodging the complacent and redirecting the wayward.				
TOTAL				

D. Giving

	3 MUCH	2 SOME	1 LITTLE	0 NONE
1. I have often given things or money cheerfully for the Lord's work.				
2. I feel deeply moved when confronted with urgent financial needs in God's work.				

	3 MUCH	2 SOME	1 LITTLE	0 NONE
3. I am so confident that God will meet my needs that I give to Him sacrificially.				
TOTAL				
E. *Mercy*				
1. I would enjoy taking shut-ins for a drive or helping them in other areas.				
2. I enjoy visiting hospitals and would do well in such a ministry.				
3. I have felt an unusual compassion for those with physical or spiritual needs.				
TOTAL				
F. *Hospitality*				
1. I feel I could provide food and/or lodging graciously to those in need.				

	3 MUCH	2 SOME	1 LITTLE	0 NONE
2. I have provided a gracious home for guests without the feeling of family interruption.				
3. I have a genuine graciousness toward the guests who come to my home.				
TOTAL				

G. *Leadership*

	3 MUCH	2 SOME	1 LITTLE	0 NONE
1. I have influenced others to accomplish a particular task or biblical purpose.				
2. I would enjoy leading, inspiring, and motivating others to involve themselves in the Lord's work.				
3. I have the desire to persuade others to move toward achieving biblical objectives.				
TOTAL				

	3 MUCH	2 SOME	1 LITTLE	0 NONE

H. Ministry

1. I would enjoy being called upon to do a special job around the church.

2. I feel satisfaction in performing routine tasks for God's glory.

3. I have been able to identify and meet the needs involved in a task in the Lord's work.

TOTAL

Evaluation

1. Which of the eight gifts did you score highest on?

   (1) _____ (2) _____ (3) _____

2. What sense of competence might you experience when the Holy Spirit develops this gift?

   _____

3. In doing this gift well, what might it do for your need to feel appreciated?

   _____

Spiritual Gift Definitions

A. Prophecy. The gift of prophecy is the special ability to receive and communicate divinely inspired revelations.

B. Teaching. The gift of teaching is the special ability to communicate precepts by word, example, or experience to the body of Christ in such a way that others will learn.

C. Exhortation. The gift of exhortation is the special ability to minister words of comfort, warning, encouragement, and advice to other members of the body so that they feel helped and healed.

D. Giving. The gift of giving is the special ability to contribute material resources to the work of the Lord liberally and cheerfully.

E. Mercy. The gift of mercy is the special ability that God gives to demonstrate genuine empathy/compassion and kindness for individuals who suffer distressing circumstances.

F. Hospitality. The gift of hospitality is the special ability that God gives to provide an open house and a warm welcome to those in need of food and lodging.

G. Leadership. The gift of leadership is the special ability that God gives to set goals in accordance with God's purpose for the future and to give direction and guidance toward their fulfillment.

H. Ministry. The gift of ministry is the special ability that God gives to identify the unmet needs, to make use of available resources to meet those needs, and help accomplish the desired results.

Appendix B

Recommended Reading for Continued Emotional and Spiritual Growth

Rich Buhler, *Pain and Pretending* (Nashville: Thomas Nelson, 1988).

John Bradshaw, *Healing the Shame That Binds You* (Deerfield Beach, FL: Health Communications, Inc., 1988)

Clarke and Dawson, *Growing Up Again* (Hazelden Press, 1989).

Dr. Robert Hemfelt and Dr. Paul Warren, *Kids Who Carry Our Pain* (Nashville: Thomas Nelson, 1990).

Dr. Robert Hemfelt, Dr. Frank Minirth, and Dr. Paul Meier, *Love Is a Choice* (Nashville: Thomas Nelson, 1989).

Dr. Robert Hemfelt, Dr. Sharon Sneed, Dr. Frank Minirth, and Dr. Paul Meier, *Love Hunger* (Nashville: Thomas Nelson, 1990).

Harriet Lerner, *The Dance of Anger* (New York: Harper & Row, 1985).

Leanne Payne, *The Healing Presence* (Wheaton, IL: Crossway Books, 1989).

Leanne Payne, *Crisis in Masculinity* (Wheaton, IL: Crossway Books, 1985).

Woititz and Garner, *Lifeskills for Adult Children* (Deerfield Beach, FL: Health Communications, 1990).

Oswald Chambers, *My Utmost For His Highest* (New York: Dodd Mead, 1935).

Hannah Hurnard, *Hind's Feet On High Places* (Wheaton, IL: Tyndale House, 1977).

Miles J. Stanford, *The Green Letter* (Grand Rapids, MI: Zondervan, 1975).

A. W. Tozer, *The Knowledge of the Holy* (Bromley, Great Britain: STL Publications, 1961).

Appendix C

Forms for "Finding the Time to Be a Woman of God"

Weekly Schedule for Being a Woman of God

	SUNDAY	MONDAY	TUESDAY	WEDNESDAY	THURSDAY	FRIDAY	SATURDAY
6 a.m.							
7							
8							
9							
10							
11							
12 noon							
1							
2							
3							
4							
5							
6							
7							
8							
9							
10							

Long-Term Goals

AREA:

GOAL:

Activities for Reaching the Goal:

Ten-Year Goal Activities:

Five-Year Goal Activities:

One-Year Goal Activities:

Weekly Goal Activities:

YEARLY PLANNING WORKSHEET

Yearly Planning Worksheet (Sample)

Yearly Goal	Activities	Schedule
Spiritual:		
Physical:		
Mental:		
Social:		

Notes

Chapter 2

1. W. R. Newell in Miles J. Stanford, *The Green Letters* (Grand Rapids, MI: Zondervan, 1975), 21.

Chapter 3

1. Lawrence J. Crabb, Jr., *Understanding People* (Grand Rapids, MI: Zondervan, 1987), 164.

Chapter 4

1. John Leonard, *Pocket Pal* (Teaneck, NJ: Design House, Inc., 1992), 65.

2. Alan Loy McGinnis, *The Friendship Factor* (Minneapolis, MN: Augsburg Publishing House, 1979), 9.

Chapter 5

1. Leanne Payne, *Crisis in Masculinity* (Wheaton, IL: Crossway, 1985), 98.

2. Leanne Payne, *The Healing Presence* (Wheaton, IL: Crossway, 1989), 56.

Chapter 7

1. Dan Stanford, *Pocket Pal* (Teaneck, NJ: Design House, Inc., 1992), 7.

Chapter 8

1. Doris Mortman, *Pocket Pal* (Teaneck, NJ: Design House, Inc., 1992), 75.

Chapter 9

1. Benjamin R. De Jong, *Uncle Ben's Quotebook* (Eugene, OR: Harvest House Publishers, 1976), 227.

Chapter 10

1. Mignon McLaughlin, *Pocket Pal* (Teaneck, NJ: Design House, Inc., 1992), 47.

2. Paul Tournier, *To Understand Each Other* (Richmond, VA: John Knox, 1967), 11.

3. David L. Luecke, *Prescription for Marriage* (Columbia, MD: The Relationship Institute, 1989), 3.

4. Ibid.

5. Dr. Ronald Hawkins, *Strengthening Marital Intimacy* (Lynchburg, VA: Liberty University Home Study Program, 1990), 27.

6. Murray Bowen, *Family Therapy* (Monterey, CA: Brooks/Cole Publishing, 1985), 170.

7. David L. Luecke, 6.

Chapter 11

1. John Bradshaw, *Healing the Shame That Binds You* (Deerfield Beach, FL: Health Communications, Inc., 1988), 18.

Chapter 12

1. Edith Schaeffer, *The Tapestry* (Waco, TX: Word Books, 1981).

About the Author

Ginger Gabriel is an author and speaker, as well as a Marriage, Family, Child Counselor (MFCC) intern, working under the supervision of Walter Linn, Ph.D., license #MFC16431, with Genesis Counseling Services in San Bernardino, California. She has been on the staff of Campus Crusade for Christ for twenty-eight years in several countries. Her unique background as a Teaching Director for Community Bible Study, a missionary, and a biblical counselor enables her to direct the Word of God toward emotional and spiritual healing.

Ginger earned her B.A. in English from Cal-State University at Long Beach, her M.A. in Missions from the International School of Theology, and her M.A. in Counseling from Liberty University in Virginia. She is also a homemaker, mother of three, and wife of Dr. Stanford Gabriel.